Guidelines To

Teaching

Remedial Reading

A Holistic Approach

(Third Edition)

by

Lillie Pope

BOOK LAB PO Box 206, Ansonia Station, New York, NY 10023

Published by:

BOOK LAB
PO Box 206, Ansonia Station
New York, NY 10023-0206
Telephone: 212 874-5534 - 800 654-0481
Fax: 212 874-3105
E mail: booklabpub@aol.com

Book # 2500 (ISBN # 87594-354-3)

Text design and production:
Maurice Leon and Karen Katz

Cover design:
Larry Noel

Graphics:
Irving Glucksman

Printed in the United States of America

To

Daniel Ezra, Raphael and Abigil Tao Yu

I thank Deborah Edel for invaluable assistance and suggestions, Ruth Dropkin for support and assistance when this book was first written, and I thank my husband for his patience.

This book was originally written as a guide for tutors involved in compensatory education programs. Experience has shown that the book may also be used advantageously by classroom teachers for group or class instruction.

Table of Contents

Tidbits

Poor basic skills are evident in 69% of all those arrested, 85% of unwed mothers, 85% of dropouts, and 72% of the unemployed.

J.A. Berlin and A. Sum, *Toward More Perfect Union: Basic Skills, Poor Families and Our Economic Future*, The Ford Foundation, 1988

• • • • • • • • • • •

"This one drug dealer said to me, 'the scariest thing to a kid out here on the street is not drugs, AIDS, guns, jail, death. It's words on a page. Because if a 15-year-old kid could handle words on a page, he'd be home doing his homework instead of selling dope with me.'"

New York Times, Sunday, September 6, 1992

• • • • • • • • • • •

"The total time parents spend with their children has diminished by about one-third and perhaps even one-half in the past thirty years. Not only are mothers home much less but there is little evidence that fathers spend more time with their children to compensate. Only about 5 percent of American children see a grandparent regularly. They spend a vast amount of time during their years of most rapid growth and development gazing at the mixture of reality and fantasy presented by television, hanging out in a variety of out-of-home settings, or taking care of themselves (which often means no care at all). Adolescents increasingly are immersed in a separate 'teen culture,' lacking adult leadership, mentorship, and support."

David A. Hamburg, President, Carnegie Corporation of New York, "Children of Urban Poverty: Approaches to a Critical American Problem," 1992, p. 4.

• • • • • • • • • • •

Did you know that, for 32 million Americans over the age of five, English is a second language? This was the report of the

1990 Census. As you read these words, the figure is undoubtedly larger, for the number of immigrants has increased rapidly since the 1990 census. This figure does not include illegal immigrants, who are uncounted. Spanish is the most common first language; the Asian language population shows the most rapid rise (Chinese, Tagalog, Korean, Vietnamese, Japanese, Thai, Mon-Khmer), as does the French Creole. German, Italian, Polish, Greek, Yiddish, Hungarian, and Dutch were spoken less frequently at home in 1990 than in 1980.

New York Times, April 28, 1993

• • • • • • • • • • •

Would you believe that 43 commonly used English words account for half of the words actually spoken in English, and that nine account for fully a quarter of all spoken words? The Big Nine are **and**, **be**, **have**, **it**, **of**, **the**, **to**, **will**, and **you**. These nine words account for one quarter of the words in written English as well.

George H. McKnight, *English Words and Their Background,* Appleton-Century-Crofts, 1969

▬ ▪ ▬ ▪ ▬ ▪ ▬ ▪ ▬

You will enjoy this poem:

Hints On Pronunciation For Foreigners

I take it you already know
Of tough and bough and cough and dough?
Others may stumble but not you
On Hiccough, thorough, laugh and through.
Well done! And now you wish, perhaps,
To learn of less familiar traps?

Beware of heard, a dreadful word
That looks like beard, and sounds like bird,
And dead: it's said like bed, not bead—
For goodness' sake don't call it "deed"!

Watch out for meat and great and threat
(They rhyme with suite and straight and debt.)

A moth is not a moth in mother
Nor both in bother, broth in brother,
And here is not a match for there
Nor dear and fear for bear and pear.
And then there's dose and rose and lose—
Just look them up—and goose and choose.
And cork and work and card and ward,
And font and front and word and sword,
And do and go and thwart and cart—
Come, come, I've hardly made a start!
A dreadful language? Man alive.
I'd mastered it when I was five.

From a letter published in the *London Sunday Times*
(January 3, 1965)

Preface

There are, unfortunately, too many individuals handicapped by lack of skill in reading, writing and arithmetic. Estimates vary on the number of adults in this country who cannot read well enough to deal with agreements, instructions, contracts and who cannot read the simple books that their children bring home from school. It is conservatively estimated that 27 million adults in this country are illiterate and the number is growing by two million each year.*

Of great concern is the fact that, in addition, for many reasons, many children in the schools are now also failing to learn, and will, unless we help them, become part of this vast army of the illiterate.

All predictions agree that the work force of the future will rely more on literacy skills than ever before in history; the illiterate will have great difficulty in getting jobs that are self-supporting, and will in addition suffer great discomfort and poor self-esteem.

It is not too late to learn. Proper instruction can help the adult, the school dropout, and the children in school who need and want help in breaking the barrier to literacy and dignity.

Because the supply of trained remedial teachers is limited, tutors can be helpful. Tutors may be paid, or they may be volunteer workers in programs that have been set up in or outside the schools. But tutors who lack adequate guidance may fail with their students just as the regular educational system has failed with them.

This book embodies a holistic approach to reading instruction. This approach is based upon the premise that there is an interdependance of the processing of information through all the senses, and the interest and experience of the learner.

This book deals with the specific techniques needed for teaching children, adolescents, and adults to read; it discusses the nature of the relationship between the tutor and the student; it outlines in simple terms the skills that are involved in the act of reading; it shows the tutor how to evaluate the student's reading level and determine his strengths and weaknesses. Finally, the tutor is guided in organizing an effective program of instruction and is provided with helpful tips and suggestions for materials useful in providing reading instruction in a program limited in funds.

Information Please Almanac, Atlas and Yearbook, 1991, Boston, Houghton-Mifflin

These procedures have been used successfully for more than thirty years by thousands of tutors with many thousands of students. The tutors have been old and young, experienced and novices, housewives, grandparents, parents, teachers and other school personnel, persons in the helping professions, peer-tutors, and dedicated volunteers who fit none of the above categories. Not only have they been able to help the thousands of students with whom they met, but many report that they themselves have gained much from the process. The virtue of this book lies in the simplicity with which it presents sophisticated theoretical and background material without jargon, stripping the mystique from the field. In short, this is a "hands-on," "how-to" book, based on solid educational success, that equips the teacher or teacher-surrogate with the material to teach with confidence and assurance of success.

Try it. You should find it very helpful.

Introduction

The people you will be teaching have been battered by frustration and failure; their self-esteem has been assaulted because they have been unable to learn what, in their view, others learn so easily. They need success. They need a resurgence of joy in learning—the joy in learning with which the child is born, and which is so often squelched by failure upon failure.

Most of you will be working with students who require remediation, students who have failed to master the reading process, but who have probably learned little bits and pieces that don't come together yet to open the door to reading. Each of these persons—child or adult—needs an individualized approach: the spark of love of learning must be cultivated in each one, and each one must be assisted in learning what s/he lacks, while the bits and pieces that they already know must be acknowledged. Each one must be kept interested in the reading matter. There should be no factory belt line for these learners.

Reading instruction in the twentieth century has been replete with polarization. In a sense, that is good, because it is a measure of the passion invested by teachers in their work. My own stance is more temperate: my experience has been that success in teaching depends to a large degree on the quality of the teachers and the climate for learning set up in the classroom. Most successful are those who are open-minded, not rigid, but flexible and prepared to adapt their teaching to the individual needs of their students. Every method, in the hand of the enthusiastic, knowledgeable, hard-working teacher, has met with many successes. I will speak briefly about two approaches that are not mutually exclusive. One is the Whole Language Approach, the other is the teaching of skills.

THE WHOLE LANGUAGE APPROACH AND THE TEACHING OF SKILLS

In many schools today, you will find a wonderful approach and a wonderful climate: the Whole Language Approach, which is intended to cultivate joy in learning, just as you intend to do with your remedial student. The Whole Language Approach provides a climate in which the learner is encouraged, through the presence of many varied books and activities, to explore and learn. All the language arts—reading, writing, listening and speaking—are emphasized and integrated. The learners read many books, and write a lot; they are encouraged also to speak and to listen. In this setting, many students learn to read easily, and become avid readers: they learn to love books. This works well for the "emergent reader," the beginning reader, the budding reader—and for the advanced reader as well—for the readers who are and have been successful in learning to read. They read easily and meaningfully, and they express themselves easily and well, both in writing and in speaking. As a result, these readers learn to think critically.

You, however, will usually be working with the "emergent illiterate", one who has failed many times, and is doomed to illiteracy unless he receives special assistance. In addition to the above, you will therefore wish to provide assistance with the skills that this person has obviously not been able to master on his own. Since reading is a language skill, you will approach the teaching of reading, writing, speaking and listening with flexibility, creativity, and close attention to the needs and response of the student, so that your teaching responds to his needs and interests.

GO FORTH AND SLAY DRAGONS!

How to Use This Book

A. BEFORE YOU MEET YOUR STUDENT

1. Read Part 1 carefully.
2. Skim through Parts 2 and 3 to acquaint yourself with the type of information available.

B. After you meet your student

1. Get to know your student and his interests.
2. Determine the student's reading level. See page 86.
3. Determine your student's reading requirements
   a. If at the third grade level or below:
      Target skills are described on page 88.
      Suggestions for correcting bad reading habits, page 141.
      Applicable word lists, see pages 156 ff.
      Useful games, see page 148.
      Additional materials, see pages 200 ff.
   b. If at the fourth to eighth grade reading level:
      Target skills are described on page 127.
      Suggestions for correcting bad reading habits, page 141.
      Applicable word lists, see pages 156 ff.
      Useful games, see page 148.
      Additional materials, see pages 200 ff.
   c. If at the ninth grade level or above:
      Target skills are described on page 131.
      Suggestions for correcting bad reading habits, page 141.
      Word lists, see pages 156 ff.
      Additional materials, see pages 200 ff.
      GED High School Equivalency Exam, see page 137.
4. Plan Your Instruction!
      Sample lesson plan, see page 145.

A Note on Gender

Many more boys than girls have difficulty learning to read. Although many hypotheses have been proposed to explain this discrepancy, we have no proven, scientific explanation. Some suggest that the causes are mainly cultural, while others favor biological explanations. Whatever the cause, the teacher or tutor working in the elementary, intermediate and high schools will be working with more boys than girls.

Students in adult programs and in classes where English is a second language, in contrast, number more women than men. This imbalance is easier to explain. Most classes are held during the day, when men are working or seek work. In the evening, men who have been working are too tired to attend class, and perhaps, since they are already working, are not motivated to improve their skills.

In order to be fair to male and female in this book, since you will be working with both, I have used pronouns in the following manner, with which I hope you will be comfortable:

instead of **she** or **he**: I have used **s/he**
instead of **him**, **his**, **her**, **her's**: I have used **him**, **his** in Part **I**, and **her**, **her's** in the remainder of the book.

Part I

Background:
Before You Begin

Before You Begin

The most important tool for learning is reading. This manual concentrates on instruction in remedial reading and can therefore be used to assist a tutor participating in any type of remedial education program. Since you are giving your time and energy, you want to do a good job. You will therefore have to know your subject and your student; you will also have to know how to impart your knowledge to the student. The reasons for his failure are complex; you must assume that your student is not stupid and that he can learn. You must also remember that the teacher has no magic formulas; the teacher can help the student open the door to learning, but the student must walk through. Your confidence in his capability to create a fuller life for himself, your confidence that more rewarding job opportunities and more pleasure in life will be available to him, must be transmitted to him.

The student will have many doubts and hesitations. You must convince him that there is hope and that by improving his reading skills, he can make tomorrow a better day than today.

In the following pages, we will try to help you do your job. We suggest that you read through the whole manual before you meet your student or students. After you have met your students, you should reread the manual, paying special attention to the sections that deal specifically with students like yours; mark the portions to which you will want to refer.

Teaching can be a rewarding experience for you. Be patient. As your student learns, you too will learn.

Why Students Come to Reading Programs

Some are sent by their teachers, some by parents, and some by agencies that feel that greater skill in reading will be helpful to them. Others come on their own, having their doubts, yet willing to try. They hope that you may help them break out of their pattern of failure. All have very specific goals, ranging from the most modest to the most challenging. Among these goals are the following:

1. To be able to keep up with studies at school.
2. To be able to read street and subway signs.
3. To gain self-respect and the respect of others.
4. To be able to function more comfortably in this country in which they are immigrants.
5. To be able to read documents requiring signature, such as leases and contracts.
6. To be able to fill out an application blank for a job.
7. To be able to read a book as other people do.
8. To learn to read the Bible.
9. To be able to help their children with their school work.
10. To learn to be better parents.
11. To seek a social outlet—to have something to do and some one to talk to.
12. To be able to read newspapers and magazines.
13. To be able to read on a higher level in order to qualify for the many types of jobs in the service occupations that require a higher reading level, or for vocational upgrading.
14. To be able to acquire the G.E.D., the high school equivalency certificate. This certificate is a minimal requirement for many jobs that represent true upgrading, and also opens the possibility of higher education.

To help your student master his difficulties in reading, you must keep these goals in mind, the better to motivate him to learn and to sustain his interest. With heightened interest and success, with improved study habits, he will develop the ability to reach for higher levels of achievement, and to persist in working toward them. As he is successful, the student will gain an improved image of himself and a confidence in his ability to learn.

The tutor should try at all times to make reading pleasurable. Hopefully the student will learn to read well enough so that he will widen his horizons and deepen his awareness and enjoyment of life.

Why Some People Have Difficulty Learning to Read

Reading is one of the most complicated skills developed by man. To sense the impact of printed symbols on a beginning reader, try to read this:

ل⁻ך ⴸ⟊ ⅂ⴹﬡ ⅂⟊ⵜﬡ ⴸⴷ⟊ ⴺⵔⵔ ⌿⌐⌐ⴰ ⵜﬡⴵ

⅂⌐ ⴸⴷⵜﬡ ⅂⌐ ⅂ⴹﬡ ⴺⵔⴰ ⌐ⴸ ⅂ⴹﬡ ⵜﬡⴺⴰﬡ⌐

In code, this says: *Now is the time for all good men to come to the aid of the reader.*

This example may help you understand how confusing a printed page looks to a beginner or to someone who is having trouble learning to read.

To learn to read, the individual should have the proper biological equipment with which to learn and an environment that encourages learning. Difficulties in learning can come from physical handicaps, poor environment, emotional problems, and ineffective teaching. This is what we mean:

1. **Biological Equipment.** Since reading depends so heavily on the senses of seeing and hearing, any student with a defect in either area will have special difficulty. Should you suspect that your student has a problem in vision or in hearing, inform your supervisor so that he may assist in having it corrected.

In some cases, a student may not learn because of limited intellectual capacity (sometimes called low IQ). The number of such people in the general population is small. This is true even among the group that you teach.

Some students have subtle neurological impairments that make it more difficult for them to learn to read: some have problems with receptive language or with expressing themselves, or with processing language, or with making some of the associations that are necessary in reading. You may hear the terms **dyslexic** or **learning disabled**. These people certainly benefit from supplementary assistance.

Your basic assumption must be that every student you deal with *is able* to learn more than he has already learned and that you will help him to do so.

2. **Environment.** Every child from the time of birth is exposed to the many different sounds and sights of his home and neighborhood. But the child who has been drawn into few conversations or discussions will lack the vocabulary to express his feelings or to describe many things and ideas. If, for example, no one has ever chatted with him about big and small, tomorrow and yesterday, the days of the week, or the months of the year, these concepts will be vague for him. If no one has ever read to him, or shown him pictures, or described sights outside his little world, or taken him on trips, or if there are no pencils or paper in the home, he will be handicapped as a reader.

You are in a position to help compensate for this early lack of stimulation and experience. No matter what the age of your student, child or adult, your conversation, and reading aloud can help overcome this handicap.

Students coming from a home where a foreign language is spoken may have the necessary vocabulary and concepts—but only in their mother tongue. They sometimes fail to learn to read simply because they lack familiarity with the sounds of the English language. Conversation in English is particularly important for them. (See p. __.

Children coming from homes in which education has been limited in the past, in which the book is not valued, are frequently not expected to succeed at school. This may be the attitude of the parent and, in some instances, it may be the attitude of the teacher. Unfortunately, such children can easily absorb the feeling that learning is not really worth the trouble it takes.

It should be remembered that people generally rise to meet expectations: your attitude should be that you expect the student to work hard and to succeed in learning what he is supposed to learn. Your attitude will have a beneficial effect on his attitude toward learning.

3. **Emotional Problems.** Emotional factors are inevitably intertwined with reading difficulties. Even when they are not the primary cause of the reading difficulty, emotional problems are bound to develop in every case of reading failure. Reading failure is school failure,

and because the school is generally important in present-day life, the emotional ill effects of school failure spread to other aspects of an individual's performance.

The student who fails can easily come to believe that he is stupid, that he is inadequate, and that he is worthless. His behavior reflects these feelings and serves as a further deterrent to learning. He is unable to pay attention and becomes restless and impatient. He may seek some other interest or outlet for his energies, and become disruptive in class.

Problem readers are thus all too often seen as "bad" children, and *they see themselves* as "bad" children. They are impatient, unable to wait for things they want; a desire for something is translated into immediate physical movement. Despite their apparent competence and confidence in some situations, such children suffer from a lack of self-esteem. Convinced that they are hopeless failures, they lose all confidence that they can learn, despite the bravado of some who insist that they know it all, or that they don't care. As they grow older, reading backwardness dooms them to continued failure in school. As their feelings of misery pile up, they are absent more and more, and finally many of them give up and drop out altogether.

4. **Inadequate Schooling.** Inadequate, insufficient and inappropriate teaching accounts for some cases of failure to learn to read. In some cases, the teaching is appropriate for many of the students in the class, who make good progress, but is inappropriate for the few who fail to learn with the methodology in this classroom, but who would do well with a different approach, and if their learning needs were attended to. In addition, reading English has a number of quirks that make it difficult for some to learn. See pages 62-64, 67 ff.

Also, even in this day and age, some students will come to you who have never had the opportunity to go to school. This last group cannot be called failures. They can learn quickly, once you convince them that it is not too late to start.

Since a cause is rarely simple or isolated, it is probable that a combination of the foregoing factors has contributed to the failures of the students with whom you will deal.

Because of this chain of failures, these students are deprived of the opportunity to enrich their lives through rewarding jobs and the pleasurable use of leisure time. As they grow older, they become dependent on others for the interpretation of the written word. In cases where the text is a contract for an installment-plan purchase or a lease, the disabled reader is an easy prey for exploitation by the dishonest.

Qualities Needed in the Tutor

You are now working in a professional capacity as an auxiliary staff member. You are working with a **team** of professionals who will appreciate your dedication to the program. Much of the success of the program will depend on your good judgment and your ingenuity. You will be expected to have:

1. Respect for your students.
2. Absolute confidence in their ability to learn.
3. Acceptance of the student as a person. Never scold, never reproach You are there to help him learn to read; he has not applied to you for therapy or for "remaking" as a person.
4. Flexibility. Each thing may be taught in many ways; try to create many ways yourself, remembering to present new material in novel and interesting ways that appeal to the senses of sight, hearing and touch. Inquire into the methods and techniques of other teachers, and borrow what is useful to you.
5. Adaptability. You must always work cheerfully with your student, despite the inconveniences of noise, lack of privacy, inadequate equipment, and insufficient and inappropriate materials. Improvise: large sheets of white paper will substitute for a chalkboard; a screen will serve as a partition.
6. Knowledge of the skills to be taught, or readiness to learn those skills. Your reading of this manual, for example, indicates a readiness to learn these skills.
7. Commitment to the program of tutoring. This requires a definite commitment of time. If you are entering this program on trial, with the feeling that you may have to drop out if you do not enjoy it or for some other reason, indicate this to the director of the program. He will then take this into account in assigning you.
8. Ability to maintain an ethical, professional relationship with the student. His confidences must at all times be respected. The student must never be discussed with anyone but the program super-

visor. Much harm can be done in casual talk or gossip. This point cannot be repeated too frequently.

9. Model behavior. The tutor is not expected to be perfect. He is, however, expected to serve as model for the behavior of the student. Remember that until now your student has learned largely by observation and imitation. By virtue of the tutor's punctuality, courtesy, speech, and appropriate dress, the student learns what is expected of him; it is not necessary to discuss such things with him explicitly. If he learns to respect the tutor, he will adopt him as a model. Sometimes the gains may not be apparent until long after you have terminated instruction.

What You Should Know About Good Teaching

PRINCIPLES OF TEACHING AND LEARNING

The following principles of teaching and learning are helpful in teaching any student. They are essential in dealing with the special needs of students who require individual instruction because they are "emergent illiterates,"—that is, they have failed to learn to read in the past, and, without special intervention, will remain illiterate

1. Remember that each individual is different.

Though students are similar in many ways, each one is unique, with individual strengths and weaknesses. Each one can best be helped by comparing him and his progress to himself, not his brothers or sisters or parents or classmates.

2. The human being learns by doing.

An old Chinese proverb:

I hear and I forget,
I see and I remember,
I do and I understand.

Information is sent to the brain by each of the senses; we learn by seeing, hearing, touching, moving our muscles, tasting, and smelling. If any of the senses fail, or if they lead the individual astray, a person will have special problems in learning. Thus, the blind have serious problems in learning, as do the deaf. Some people, though they have adequate vision, have some subtle difficulty in receiving and interpreting information that they receive through the eyes—and consequently have special learning problems. Others have problems with information that they receive through their sense of hearing—they also have problems in learning. These problems can be overcome with careful, attentive instruction.

In the traditional classroom, where children sit at their desks most of the day and listen to the teacher, the students are exposed mainly to an oral type of instruction. They are expected to learn primarily by means of hearing, and secondarily by looking. Nowadays, many classrooms are set up with activity centers; students move from one activity to another; they explore, and learn by doing.

Individual tutorial instruction has the great advantage of permitting the student to learn through all of his senses, using a "multi-sensory approach." One can listen, look, touch, feel, move around and learn by way of the muscles, and one can also taste and smell. The student can learn by doing—the most effective way of learning any skill. Imagine learning how to drive a car, or how to swim, by listening to a lecture that describes all of the movements to be learned. Obviously only by "doing"—using muscles, touch and feel, using vision as well as by hearing—can these skills be learned properly. This also holds true for learning to read.

If the student has difficulty in understanding information that comes in via one sensory channel, s/he may receive and understand more efficiently through another one of the senses. Remember that one can learn a lot through the muscles, and moving around helps release the student's pent-up energy. If one is learning the letter "t" for example, one can write it in the air, shape it with one's body, shape it out of clay, feel it on sandpaper, trace it on acetate, trace it in sand, write it on the chalkboard (with the large muscles), write it on paper (with the small muscles), eat an alphabet cracker shaped "t" after feeling it with one's finger, shape it out of licorice, and then eat it, and say a word beginning with the sound as one performs each of these tasks. Although this sounds like a simple task, for some learners it is difficult at first.

Not only is it easier for the individual to learn when information comes in through all of the senses—but it is more enjoyable. Restless students can move around; multi-sensory materials are more colorful and more interesting than the incessant bombardment of being "talked-at." And the pleasures and successes of learning-by-doing provide more satisfaction to the student who has had difficulty keeping up with the work in the large classroom and has "tuned out" on what was happening there.

The multi-sensory approach can be tailored to the individual's needs and interests; it recognizes and respects the fact that each individual is different and merits a different approach and materials.

3. The interest of the student must be captured at all times.

If the student is not interested, s/he will not learn. Though the student may be reluctant about reading, the time you spend together should be centered around some area in which s/he is interested. This may be baking or cooking for one student, dinosaurs for another, policemen, firemen, drug abuse, horse racing or South Africa for others. The interest of the recent immigrant may be in how to cope with the demands of daily life in this new world: shopping, handling money and/or food stamps, dealing with social agencies. The skills in reading can then be related to this area of interest. The student can talk about the subject, do research on the subject with the tutor, become involved in activities related to the subject, dictate stories about it, write about it, read about it—and learn reading skills at his own level—but related to his area of interest. The student will at the same time learn how to find out things for himself.

4. Make reading pleasurable to the student.

Spend some time at each session reading to the student: select a joke, a short story, a recipe, or some book that fascinates him. Help him associate a feeling of pleasure with the printed word.

Games are helpful in teaching many of the reading skills, and also make the session enjoyable for the student. Many tutors are reluctant to play reading games because they take so much time; the tutors are impatient for the student to learn quickly what s/he failed to learn during the years of prior instruction. Enjoyable tasks that are related to reading skills help the student learn more quickly than monotonous, tedious teaching—from which the student fails to learn. Use games—and be patient.

5. Choose your words carefully.

In the traditional classroom, the teacher talks much of the time—and the student is required to listen. The failing student has difficulty paying attention to the constant stream of "teacher talk," and so s/he "tunes it out"—and stops listening.

This is a powerful lesson to the person who deals with the student on a one-to-one basis. Be careful not to talk too much, or the student will "tune" you out too. Be certain that the student is encouraged to talk, and that there is lots of "doing" during the session.

When you speak, keep your language at the level of the student. Avoid using concepts and idioms that s/he cannot understand. If s/he has a foreign-language background, be certain that s/he understands the words that you use. Some individuals tend to be very literal in their thinking. Thus, if you say, "When I heard that, I fell apart," or "my head started to spin," they look for the body that has fallen into several disconnected pieces, or they look for the head that is spinning. If your student tends to think in this fashion, try to avoid using idioms, phrases, and words that will disconcert him. Explain the meaning of each expression that seems to confuse him. Help him to use it too. It is possible to speak simply, clearly and respectfully without "talking down" to the student. You will be able to do it.

6. Encourage oral expression: avoid asking questions that call for "yes" or "no" answers.

Reading is a language skill. Therefore improvement in oral expression is an important goal in your work with the student with reading problems. When you converse with him, try to encourage him to express himself easily, in a relaxed way. With increased practice in verbal expression, one can improve his vocabulary, formulate his experiences and his thoughts in an orderly way, and thus use language for more effective communication. When you converse with him, enable him to express himself by being certain that you do not talk too much and do not ask him questions that can be answered by the words "yes" or "no"; they do not encourage expression. Instead of asking "Did you like the _____ show last night on T.V.?" ask, "What did you think of the _____ show?" or "Tell me what the show was about."

7. Plan for many activities within the period.

Most students who have failed are restless. They are also unable to pay attention to one thing for more than a short period of time. It is important to hold the student's attention by preparing many activities for each session. No activity should last more than five minutes; for a session lasting forty minutes, be prepared with at least eight activities. These activities may be designed to teach the same thing—approached from several different angles—or they may have different goals. For example, in teaching the letter "t" as described earlier, each varied activity lasts just long enough to hold the student's attention. Because of the restlessness of the student, it is helpful to plan the activities in such a way that the student has the opportunity to leave his seat and move around between sedentary tasks.

Learn the art of shifting to a new activity before the student wearies of the old one.

Remember that one of the activities for each session should be your reading something of great interest and enjoyment for the student; a discussion or chat about his special interests or concerns is important, interesting to the student, and helpful in encouraging him to express himself.

8. Plan each lesson, and keep notes.

Your notes and your lesson plans will remind you of what your student knew when you began. They will help you plan clearly for each lesson, and will also make it easier for your supervisor to help guide you, and for a substitute to step in for you when you are sick or called away by an emergency. Your notes will also remind you of important details that are so easy to forget if they are not written down: the student's nickname, his birthday, problems that s/he has mentioned that should be shared with the supervisor.

Remember that it is your responsibility to plan carefully for the lesson, and at the same time to be flexible, taking your cues on content from the student. Build on your student's strengths and interests. The girl who likes to cook will learn to read recipes, though she may resist formal reading instruction.

It is important to plan for the student to make some progress each day, and to know what success he is having. Without some planning, failures and frustration result. These are disastrous for your students who have experiences these F's so many times in the past. On the other hand, be careful not to overwhelm or overburden the student. He must leave each lesson with a real sense of enjoyment and achievement.

Keep an accurate attendance record. It will help you later when you try to evaluate his progress, and yours.

These records should be kept in a file in the supervisor's office, and should be available only to the supervisor and the tutors. Their privacy must be respected

9. Use tactile, colorful materials.

Whenever possible, use materials that can be handled and manipulated. Because students learn best "by doing," the use of materials that make it possible for them "to do" helps them learn more easily. Materials of different textures and of attractive colors are stimulating to the senses and to the imagination—and make each activity more memorable. Your imagination and the discards in your wastebasket will produce the kinds of materials that can be used, for example, in the shaping and tracing of the letters and words (and the numbers), or in the mounting of their written material, and making books that they write and/or illustrate. The following materials that come to mind can be used imaginatively: crayon, paint, acetate, felt, velvet, sand, magic markers, felt-tipped pens, sandpaper, cookies, pipe-cleaners, licorice, magazine pictures, construction paper, tissue paper, crepe paper, cloth of different colors and textures, wool. You can list ten more in the margin of this page.

10. Be clear about your rules—about what is permitted and what is not permitted.

Your student will welcome knowing what to expect, what one may do, and what one is not allowed to do. In other words, let him know "the rules of the game," and stick to them. Some things are never allowed: the student is never permitted to hurt another person, or to destroy equipment. Some of the rules may be imposed by the school, and some may be yours: one is not permitted to run and shout in the corridor, one is not permitted to come to the tutorial session early, while you are tutoring the preceding student. You may find it helpful to restrict the number of times one takes a drink of water during the session, or the number of times one goes to the toilet. The rules should be clear, and you must be consistent about adhering to them.

The student is more secure when he knows how his "world" operates. Let him know what to expect from you.

11. Don't promise what you can't deliver.

In order for the student to have confidence in you, s/he must know that you always keep your word, and that your promises are made in good faith. Therefore, be cautious; promise only those things that you know you can deliver. It is poor practice to promise something that depends on another individual. That third person may very well fail to deliver to you, and then you in turn will disappoint your student. Thus, if you plan to lend him a book that you like, promise it only if you yourself have it at home and will bring it in. Do not promise it if you plan to borrow it from the library. It may not be at the library when you stop there to pick it up; as a result, you will have failed to keep your word.

12. Focus on your goal; do not criticize irrelevancies.

Your primary goal is to help the student learn how to read. You will discover that s/he has many, many problems in addition to those of learning how to read. He may come in without a handkerchief or tissues, and his speech may be different from yours. He may say "ain't" and his vocabulary may be earthy. His fingernails may be dirty, and his clothing soiled. Do not criticize any of these—concentrate only on the reading. If this is a young child, and you inquire about his clothing and his cleanliness, he will interpret that as a reflection on his family and his background—and his self-esteem will be further injured. Accept him as he is. Respect him for his positive qualities and concentrate solely on the subject matter at hand.

If you find that the student has other problems that are urgent, discuss them with the program supervisor who will then attend to them. In this way, disruptive personal problems will be taken care of as well as can be in this shaky world, and your relationship with the student will remain uncomplicated.

13. Keep your schedule of lessons regular and evenly spaced.

Psychologists tell us that we will learn more quickly if our lessons are evenly spaced throughout the week, rather than having them concentrated in one day. For example, if we have two hours a week to devote to learning a skill such as typewriting, then it is inefficient to concentrate the lesson into two hours in one day a week. Planning for two hours of typing every Monday is a poor way to set up instruction; twenty minutes a day for six days a week will permit the best learning. Investing the same number of minutes per week, the student has less fatigue daily, and less time between lessons to forget what was learned at the previous lesson. Though six periods of reading instruction may not be practical for many people, the instruction should be planned for as many sessions a week as possible. Learning will be very slow and frustrating if the student has fewer than two sessions each week.

14. Provide for much repetition and practice—but not boredom

Memory and learning are closely related. The student with learning problems often forgets more easily than do most people. Every point in this "check list" is directed at helping the student to remember.

Repetition and practice are essential keys to learning. Students who have failed usually need far more repetition and practice than do others.

Though the repetition and practice are essential, it is equally essential that they be presented in such a way that they are not dull. Keep the practice sessions brief and crisp. Practice the same thing in a variety of ways. If the student is trying to learn to recognize the word **that**, s/he needs practice in writing it, in reading it, in forming it with the many materials described previously (see page 30), in searching newspapers and magazines for it, in playing games that include the word, in recognizing it in flash cards. The skill may be practiced for a few minutes at every session for weeks until the student knows it automatically—that is, without having to think about it. After that time, it is important to review it regularly to be sure that s/he has not forgotten it. A skill or a bit of knowledge, if not used, is easily forgotten.

For the student who is able to read a book, even though it is at a level lower than expected for his age and grade, the best practice is provided at every session by having him read (silently) "easy" books that he selects. Such reading for pleasure helps develop fluency and confidence; these are important underpinnings for reading more difficult books.

15. Over-teach each thimbleful.

Have you been introduced to someone, known his name at the moment, and then forgotten it? Unless we use (or practice) something we have learned, it can be forgotten easily. You will be very pleased when your student reads a new sound or word correctly for the first time, but you cannot assume that s/he therefore has learned it. It is necessary that you provide more and more practice with it. This is called "over-teaching"; it is very valuable for helping the student retain what s/he has learned. On the other hand, it is also very important not to reach the point of boredom. As soon as you are satisfied that s/he knows it automatically, the special practice can be dropped. A good rule of thumb is that if the student recognizes the new sound or word automatically (without thinking about it) for three weeks in a row, then s/he has really learned it

16. Cut down on distractions as much as possible.

You will find that many of your students are very easily distracted by things that you would not notice if you were concentrating on something special. The sound of a fire-engine will draw their attention from your work. A fly, a moving object, another student, or the sight of a bright picture or shiny jewelry can draw the eye of the student away from the work at hand. To make it easier for him to concentrate during the session, it is helpful to tutor in a spot where there are few possibilities for distraction. Try to find a place that is relatively quiet. It is impossible to avoid or eliminate all noise and it is not necessary to do so. Be sure that you eliminate as many visual distractions as possible. Keep the table clear of materials that you are not using at the moment. If you must work with the student near a window, have him sit with his back to the window so that s/he will not see animals, people, or moving vehicles pass by. If you work with him in a room where there are other students, place a partition between him and the others: this can be a bookcase, or a screen. If this is difficult, s/he can sit with his back to the others.

Ideally, the physical conditions under which you teach will be such that there are few distractions. Actually, you may find the physical conditions very uncomfortable; you may be in a noisy place where people pass by frequently; the light may be poor and there may not be a chalkboard. You may even have to find yourself different corner each week. Depending on the nature of the program in which you are working, you may not be able to do much about some of these conditions. Do the best you can.

Remember that your goal is to make it easier for the student to concentrate on the material s/he is dealing with at that session. Sometimes the material on the page distracts the student from the very word or line that s/he is reading. Some students find it easier to concentrate on one word or one line if all the others are covered. Use a ruler, or a sheet of paper, or a page mask to help him concentrate, and to help keep his eyes away from all of the material that is irrelevant at the moment.

Try not to compromise on the following:
• Assure older students absolute privacy from younger children.
• Use the same location for each lesson.
• Arrange to have enough light, particularly for the student;
  if necessary bring a small table lamp for this purpose.

17. Make decisions simple by limiting the number of choices.

Most of us have difficulty making decisions. To make decisions easier for your student when you offer a choice, it is advisable to permit him to choose from only two or three possibilities. Instead of asking, "What would you like to do next?"it is better to say "Would you like to play Tic-Tac-Toe or Go-Fish?" Instead of asking "What would you like to do tomorrow?" say "Would you like to go to the museum or take a trip to the park?" In the poorly worded questions, the possibilities and choices are endless—making the decision difficult for the student. Furthermore, s/he may choose something impractical or unrealistic—and you may not be able to accommodate the request. By offering two choices, you are making the selection simple for him, and are guaranteeing that either choice is possible. You are also indicating that you respect his opinion, by accepting whichever alternative he chooses.

18. Plan for success; if the student fails, your planning is poor.

It is very important for your student that he experience success. His past experience has been that of repeated failure in learning. As one learns something successfully, one is encouraged to approach the next task with confidence that one can learn that too.

In order for him to be successful now, it is important to plan his instructional program very carefully. Each new unit must be small, and within his current grasp. It must present a small challenge, but a challenge that he can meet.

If the student fails to learn the new material, replan your lesson. Try a new approach. Analyze the task so that you may present smaller steps to the student.

19. Reward Success.

Let the student know when s/he has succeeded, even with a very small task, and encourage pleasure in that success. A reward can take many forms: it can be a smile, or a hearty response, "That was great, Jimmy;" it can be a piece of candy or a cookie or a star, or a credit that is later traded in for some prize. As the student has more and more successes s/he will need fewer external rewards, and at the same time will derive more and more pleasure from the successful learnings. Eventually the pleasure of learning will be the only reward s/he needs. In the meantime, it is important to acknowledge success.

Never compliment the student for success when s/he has not really succeeded. Sometimes a tutor will do this in order to encourage the student. This does not have the desired effect, because students know when they have not been successful, and will then recognize that the tutor is not being honest and straightforward.

However, it is essential to acknowledge and compliment the student for *trying*, even when unsuccessful.

20. Respect the privacy of confidential information.

You will be privileged to know many things about your student that are private and should be kept confidential. Many interesting bits of information will come up. Under no circumstances is it permissible to chat about them, or to gossip about them. The only person with whom information may be shared is the person who directs the program. S/he may be able to help you deal with some of the problems that arise.

Confidential information can be particularly embarrassing when the student has some personal contact with your family. For this reason, it is best to avoid working with a student who is a friend of your child, and also a student who is a child of your friend.

21. Teach at the student's level.

Much of the time the failing student is given work to do that is well beyond his level. The failing reader in the fifth grade class may be looking at a fifth grade reader that is meaningless to him. His teacher may try to be helpful by giving him a third grade reader which is also gibberish to him. The teacher may have failed to realize that the student is able to read only a few words, and does not yet know that s/he must start reading at the left side of the page and move consistently to the right. Unless his instruction starts at his present level (teaching left to right, the sounds and sight words that he lacks), s/he will continue to be a non-reader.

The student must be taught at his level. His level will vary depending on which skill we happen to be observing at the moment. Evaluate the student's skills, and help him learn those that s/he lacks, while at the same time recognizing and making use of his strengths. Only in this way can he be helped to make progress.

22. Listen; do not criticize.

As one listens to students, one is sometimes too eager to help them very quickly, and there is a tendency to interrupt, to criticize, to mention the right thing to do, and to save time. It is far more helpful to listen patiently, without criticism and with as few suggestions as possible. A friendly sympathetic listener is more helpful than a well-meaning critic and director.

There must be no suggestion of criticism of the adult or child who does not read well. Criticism may destroy self-confidence and interest in learning. Needless to say, do not ridicule the student; do not shame the student; never, never be sarcastic.

The manner in which you react to errors is very important. It is more constructive, when the student has made an error, to correct it casually, rather than to overemphasize it by asking questions to lead him to correct himself. Tell the rule, instead of asking. If it is appropriate, teach and reteach the point, but do not make an issue of the error itself.

Many of your students will have dialects and accents, making their speech different from yours. Your primary purpose is to teach reading. Too many corrections of his speech are interpreted by the student as criticism, and destroy his interest in learning. Do not correct speech. Limit your corrections to those that affect the meaning of words. This is a very subtle and difficult point: it is essential to correct only important errors. Accept the student's speech, keeping in mind that it is completely appropriate in his cultural group. Let him say "ain't", or retain his dialect or accent. Concentrate on helping him understand what he reads in English.

If you feel, however, that the student's speech is a serious handicap to him, then you should ask your supervisor whether a speech specialist is available to evaluate that problem. But you will not be helping him if you step into that area in addition to reading.

23. Maintain a professional relationship with the student.

Your relationship with the student should be friendly and respectful. Accept him as he is. Keep the relationship professional. Though you are friendly, it is helpful to keep some distance; retain your privacy, and let him retain his. The student will share many intimate thoughts and some private information with you; never pry, and never ask him for such information. When it comes, let it be because s/he wished to share with you, and because s/he trusts that you will keep it confidential.

You are not his fairy godmother or godfather. You cannot solve all of his problems. You cannot straighten out his family's marital problems, or help them make ends meet, or get him what he wants for Christmas, or find him the job that he needs or wants. When you are confronted with problems that give you concern, and that you feel someone should do something about, discuss these problems with the coordinator of the program.

It will be difficult for you to remember at all times that you are there to help him learn how to read—and that all other problems will have to be taken care of by the coordinator and those whom the coordinator can involve—or by life itself. If you maintain your focus, you will be able to help your student despite his problems.

Do not be patronizing.

Never break an appointment without notifying the student.

If a student is absent, find out why. A telephone call or a home visit may help. He may be afraid to return if he is out too long. When he returns, inquire about his health; do not reproach him.

Arrange to have your student call the office if he must miss an appointment, or will be late. This will encourage in him a feeling of responsibility to you and to the program. Do not be too disappointed if the student breaks an appointment, or if he fails to call.

If you are teaching in the neighborhood in which your students live, walk around and become familiar with it. This will help you know your student better, and will also give you something more to talk about with him.

24. Maintain a professional relationship with the teacher, if you are tutoring in a school.

The teacher is responsible for the student while s/he is at school. The teacher may feel frustrated and helpless that the student has failed to make progress or is a classroom management problem. At the same time the teacher is overwhelmed by the problem of both trying to deal with the whole class, and helping this student. Nevertheless, the arrival of a new person who may be successful with this student sometimes causes the teacher to feel threatened. The tutor must be courteous to the teacher, respect the teacher's professionalism and the difficulty that the teacher has in trying to teach 30 or 40 students at once. It is important to remember that the volunteer deals with the student in a one-to-one situation—outside of the classroom. The volunteer's work is far simpler than that of the teacher, and in no way serves as competition. The volunteer at all times serves as "supplementary" personnel—to help the teacher do what the teacher has no time to do at present. When this relationship is maintained, teachers find that they themselves are enabled to teach more effectively when they have volunteer assistance. They are happy about the progress made by individual students who receive volunteer assistance. They become enthusiastic about the program, and are eager for it to continue from year to year.

Under no circumstance should volunteer assistance be imposed on any teacher; only those teachers who request such assistance should receive it.

25. Maintain a professional relationship with the principal, your supervisor and other school personnel, if you are tutoring in a school.

The staff in your tutorial program is a team working together to help solve the problem of illiteracy. Some members of the team have more experience and training than you; some may have less. But remember, all of you are working together.

You have much to give, and much to learn; you may have questions about things you see being done, or not being done. Ask these questions of the person responsible; try to avoid jumping to conclusions; try to avoid being destructively critical and stirring up tempests. Remember that everyone involved is trying and that no one way of doing things has yet been proven to be best. Be tolerant of a certain degree of disorganization, and accept the fact that there are problems.

When you have questions about technique and problems in relation to a particular case, be sure to ask for assistance. Such requests reflect your sincere effort and interest and will earn you the respect of the staff.

It is important, when working in a school or an agency that hosts a tutorial program, to be helpful, while at the same time being invisible. The principal, teachers, clerks are all very busy, and though they would like to be courteous and thoughtful, are sometimes preoccupied with their regular duties and emergencies, and assume that you are comfortable and know your way around. They are glad to have you in the building, but they may forget to tell you some of the little details that would make life a bit easier there for you.

Be sure you know where the important points in the school are, as, for example, the principal's office, the toilets, the telephone, the fire exit, and the library. The school will provide a place for you to work, a place to hang your coat, and to keep your books.

If people seem to ignore you, it is because they are very busy. As time goes on, you will find yourself more relaxed in the building, you will be more comfortable, and they will be more hospitable.

Try to impose as little as possible on the regular school personnel. Leave no papers on the floor. Leave the furniture as you find it, and try not to use the school telephone. Though the school will be glad to help you with supplies, try to avoid burdening them with small requests. Carry your books and your plans. Keep your pencils and paper where you can find them each time—so you will not have to ask for replacements. If you can bring old magazines from home, do that instead of asking for them at school.

Though the volunteer is a great help, every extra person in the building adds a burden to the regular staff in the building—because each additional person needs space, supplies, and a host of little things. Try to make that burden as easy as possible at the beginning; as time goes on, you will be able to do things and find things for yourself. Your contribution will be well appreciated and things will go a lot more smoothly.

26. Maintain a professional relationship with the parent.

The relationship between tutor and family of the student should be courteous but impersonal. The primary relation and loyalty of the tutor is to the student. If the tutor reports to the parent or to a family member, the relationship with the student will be endangered. If the parent asks the tutor for a report on the student's progress, or wishes to discuss the student with the tutor, the parent should be referred to the person who coordinates the program at the school. In some schools, parent meetings or conferences may be arranged at which the tutorial program is described and discussed. Discussions about individual students, however, should be restricted to the special conferences arranged by the supervisor or coordinator.

If you are tutoring the student privately, however, it is still important to remember that your primary relationship and loyalty are to the student. You may wish to promise quarterly or semi-annual reports on progress to the parent; all meetings and discussions with parents must be delicately handled, and with great discretion.

27. Maintain your professionalism at home.

Your children will be very proud that you are now working in a tutorial program. Never discuss with them the problems of the students whom you tutor.

28. Maintain an awareness of the student as an individual.

Your shining goal is to help the student to become self-motivated and self-propelled. The acquisition of reading skills is just one step in the path of the student. Though you concentrate on reading in your contacts with the student, your instruction, because it is so individualized, affects his total behavior. As his attitude towards learning changes, there will be changes in his entire personality. It is not an exaggeration to say that in these changes lie most of what will have been accomplished by the tutoring process.

Again: be certain that older students are protected from the prying and sometimes unkind eyes of young children, who may ridicule them because they require remedial instruction, or because they are learning "baby" work.

29. Help your student set realistic goals.

While setting higher horizons for your student, help him maintain a realistic evaluation of his strengths and limitations. A sixteen year old boy who reads at the second grade level must continue to aspire to improve his reading, but it is not helpful to encourage him in his dreams of entering a profession that involves graduate work, such as medicine. Similarly, a boy who cannot count should not be encouraged to try to become an accountant.

30. Be confident that your student will learn.

When the teacher expects students to learn, they tend to learn quite well. On the other hand, if the teacher is forewarned that the students are dull, and therefore anticipates that they will not learn easily, the students will again meet the teacher's expectations, and fail to learn as well as the first group. There is a magical quality in expectation on the part of the teacher and of the learner; students tend to succeed or fail as expected.

Have confidence that your students will learn. Treat them with respect, and with interest. They will learn.

31. Be patient; don't be rushed. This is a long haul.

Your and your student must understand that learning after failure can in some cases be a long, slow, difficult struggle. Progress may be so slow that you may feel as though there is no movement at all. You cannot hope to teach overnight what your student has failed for years to learn. You cannot hope to undo overnight the damage that has occurred over a period of years. For this reason, it is important to keep records of exactly where the student was at the beginning of instruction—so that you may make a more realistic evaluation of his progress.

Progress may be slow for a long period of time, and then suddenly there will be a breakthrough. Hopefully, that will happen when you are still working with him, and you will have the pleasure of seeing him speed ahead. Sometimes the breakthrough comes long afterwards, and you may never know about it—or you may hear of it years later.

Review of the Principles of Teaching and Learning

✔ Remember that each individual is different.

✔ The individual learns by doing.

✔ The interest of the student must be captured at all times.

✔ Make reading pleasurable to the student.

✔ Choose your words carefully.

✔ Encourage oral expression: avoid asking questions that call for "yes" or "no" answers.

✔ Plan each lesson, and keep notes.

✔ Plan for many activities within the period.

✔ Use tactile, colorful materials.

✔ Be clear about your rules—about what is permitted and what is not permitted.

✔ Don't promise what you can't deliver.

✔ Focus on your goal; do not criticize irrelevancies.

✔ Keep your schedule of lessons regular and evenly spaced.

✔ Provide for much repetition and practice without boredom.

✔ Over-teach each thimbleful.

✔ Eliminate distractions as much as possible.

✔ Make decisions simple by limiting the number of choices.

✔ Plan for success; if the student fails, your planning is poor.

✔ Reward success.

✔ Respect the privacy of confidential information.

✔ Teach at the student's level.

✔ Listen; do not criticize.

✔ Maintain a professional relationship with the student.

✔ Maintain a professional relationship with the teacher.

✔ Maintain a professional relationship with the principal, your supervisor and other school personnel.

✔ Maintain a professional relationship with the parent.

✔ Maintain your professionalism at home.

✔ Maintain an awareness of the student as an individual.

✔ Help your student set realistic goals.

✔ Have absolute confidence that your student will learn.

✔ Be patient; don't be rushed. This is a long haul.

Tips on Techniques

SPECIFIC AIDS AND RESOURCES

About Notebooks, Files and Printing

1. Beginners find it easier to read writing and printing that is large and has ample space between the lines. You should therefore use the manuscript printing that is used in the early elementary grades. Here is what manuscript printing looks like:

This is manuscript printing

Manuscript printing is easier for the student to read because it is relatively consistent; it is helpful to use it with beginners. Be sure that you print each letter clearly and consistently each time. Since the beginning reader has great difficulty in distinguishing one letter from another, ordinary handwriting may add to his confusion.

Your everyday penmanship is called cursive writing, or script. It is usually taught in the third grade. Here it is:

This is cursive writing

2. Prepare two folders for each pupil: one will be a student's folder, and one a tutor's folder. Keep all of the student's work in his folder, neatly arranged. If you are working with a young child, have him make a drawing on the folder, to personalize it; encourage him to take pride in his work. The student may read to you his writings from the folder, and, at the end of the semester, you may send home samples of his work selected from the folder.

3. Have the student keep a hard-covered note book. If it is inappropriate for him to carry it home, or if s/he has no homework assignment, keep it in his folder between lessons. Have him work neatly in it, and take pride in its appearance. Some teachers have been very successful in having students practice on loose paper and rewrite beautifully in the hard-covered notebook, which then becomes a source of pride.

4. Prepare an individual file of word cards for each student when you teach new words, or words that the student finds difficult. Using a felt-tipped pen or heavy crayon, print one word on each card. Separate the cards into three groups: those s/he knows well (these become *Friends*; those s/he does not know (these are *Strangers*); and those s/he may know at times, but with which s/he still needs practice (these are *Acquaintances*). If possible, obtain a metal or wood box in which each student can maintain his file. Have him file the Friends alphabetically. Practice for a few minutes at each session, so that some of the Acquaintances become Friends and can be added to the file, and to enable some of the Strangers to become Acquaintances. The movement of each word into the Friends file represents a real achievement for the learner.

About the Lesson

1. Know what you are planning to do during each lesson. Try to limit each activity to five minutes. A sample plan might include:

- Present a new concept.
- Review and practice consonant blends, or words that were *Acquaintances* at the last lesson.
- Discuss coming trip to museum to see Egyptian mummies or a show of last evening.
- Write about the TV show, or about plans for the trip. Encourage the student to write this on his own; ignore spelling errors. If s/he is unable to do so, have him dictate his story to you. Have him read back the story, learn the words, and add the appropriate ones to the student's file of *Friendly* words.
- Read from book chosen by student, perhaps continued from previous lesson.
- Read to the student an anecdote, a funny story, or a newspaper item that you saved to share with him.
- Play word game, if there is time.

Another sample plan appears on page 145.

2. Try to teach something new at the beginning of each lesson, in order to maintain the student's interest. At the end of the lesson, it is very helpful to summarize what has been done that day. Include some mention of each new achievement: a word, a story read, something clarified.

Do not assume that your student remembers what s/he was taught at the last session or several sessions earlier. It is important to review the latest skills taught until you are confident that the student knows them well and is not likely to forget them. Include a five-minute review in some part of the session. Your notes on each lesson will tell you which of the skills covered last time should be reviewed today, and today's notes will remind you of what needs review at the next session.

3. Check all the written work your student does during the lesson. Do not rely on his comparing his answers with those on answer sheets provided by some publishers. A great deal of the student's learning develops as a result of the personal relationship you establish with him. When you check his work, you quickly become aware of his errors, and are in a position to clear up areas of confusion immediately. An answer sheet cannot substitute for you.

4. Find a book in which the student is interested, but that is above his reading level. (Remember that his interests and comprehension are usually beyond his reading ability.) Spend several minutes of each session reading it to him. Discuss it with him. By doing this, you are giving him pleasant associations with the printed word. At the same time, you are encouraging him to express himself, an important corollary of reading skill.

5. To further encourage a relaxed teaching atmosphere, and also to encourage the student to express himself orally, discuss television shows with your student. Have him tell you the story of a show s/he watched. Discuss magazine pictures, current events and newspaper stories with him. Assign a show of particular interest to him, and later discuss it with him.

6. At the end of each lesson make a note in your folder of what you did and your immediate thoughts on what you want to remember to do next time. Do not rely on your memory. Also note anything that the student said or did that you may want to discuss with your supervisor. In

some centers, the supervisor may have a form on which you may make these notes and reports. Where no such form is provided, it is helpful to staple to the inside cover of the tutor's folder a sheet of paper on which to make your regular notations. Always remember to date your entry. When the sheet is full, do not turn it over; staple another sheet over it, with the staples at the top of the sheet, so that you can always read all the notes by picking up the top leaves.

7. Students can help students. If you should be teaching several students at a time, you may find it helpful to have some of the students help others so that you can offer special individual assistance. When such assignments are judiciously made and carefully supervised, this can work out well.

8. Sometimes you will find your student reluctant to read aloud to you, even when you are teaching him alone. It can be very helpful, then, if you take turns reading aloud with him. Be cautious about criticizing even slight reading errors during the early phases of instruction. Since your goal is to encourage relaxation and a decrease in self-consciousness, such criticism may be self-defeating by inhibiting the student. Should s/he have difficulty with a word, supply it. If s/he has difficulty with too many words, the selection you are reading is too difficult. Shift to an easier selection.

In addition, permit the student to read silently at times, absorbing the text and enjoying the illustrations on his own. After reading it, let him tell you about it.

9. Homework must be handled sensitively. There is no hard and fast rule about assigning homework to students in remedial programs. Assignments must be optional for the student; if they are likely to destroy his interest in the instruction, avoid homework completely. If the student asks for it, give him an assignment. Be sure to check it when s/he returns. He will be very disappointed if you forget, and may fail to do the work the next time. Do not reproach him if s/he has not done it, but assign no more until s/he requests it.

10. Again, to encourage your student to express himself, as well as to enjoy the printed word:
- Read to or with your student at each session.
- Talk with your student about things that are important to him/ her.
- Send your student notes, letters, written messages.

- Help the student keep a journal, notebook or diary of thoughts and ideas.
- Tape record a book as you read it aloud so that the student can hear it again and again.
- Encourage your student, when appropriate, to create posters, models, dioramas or puppets for special occasions.
- Encourage your student to compose original stories.

About Additional Aids

1. The **public library** is an invaluable source of material for a reading program. The librarian will help you by providing interesting books and periodicals that you might not otherwise find. After she knows your needs, she will be happy to locate appropriate materials for you, and to lend books to you, for a longer-than-usual period. Take your student to the library if you can, when you find him willing to go. You may find that s/he will be very proud to own a library card of his own; help him register for one. Do not urge him to accompany you to the library if s/he seems to have unpleasant associations with it.

Your student may ask to borrow books from the program at times; if you can spare the books, it is worth lending them. Again, do not reproach him if a book is not returned. Ask for it once and no more; if a student fails to return a borrowed book, do not lend one to him again.

2. **Tabloid newspapers, comic books,** and **picture magazines** frequently appeal to your students. Use these materials, at the appropriate reading level, to teach critical evaluation of reading material. They can be very helpful in motivating your students to read, to enjoy reading, and to feel success at their present levels of instruction.

3. **Field trips** are valuable. Plan to take your student to places s/he has never visited, preferably where the admission is free. Such visits should not replace regular instruction time too often. Discuss the visits in advance, and emphasize the things to look for and expect. Afterward, have the student discuss and write about the visits, or dictate stories to you about them. Concentrate on the pleasures of the visit, and the excitement of discovering one of the many wonderful things nearby. Take care to avoid making the after-work an unpleasant burden.

Exciting places to visit include museums, zoos, theaters, concerts, the local newspaper plant, industrial plants, a firehouse, park, ferry boat, historic buildings and monuments. You will be surprised at how new all of these things will be to most of your students.

4. Encourage your student (especially the beginning reader) to read *signs* everywhere: road signs, street signs, signs on TV, advertising signs and labels, and signs at work and at school. Cut advertisements out of magazines. Boys will be particularly interested in automobile names and in traffic signs such as STOP and DETOUR. If your student is interested, make a file of these signs, treating them as you do his word file, that is, as *Friends*, *Acquaintances*, and *Strangers*.

5. **Magic Slates, felt-tipped pens and magic markers, crayons, and colored pencils** add variety and interest to written work.

6. To make your material go farther, and to make it easier to select exactly what you want, you will find it helpful to cut up **two copies of a workbook or books of reading exercises.** Staple each page to a sheet of oak tag or stiff cardboard; then file the sheets in a carton or filing cabinet. Use each sheet of practice material as needed,and then replace in the file. This permits maximum utilization of a limited amount of teaching material. An additional advantage is that this practice discourages the tutor from leaning heavily on one workbook, a procedure that is boring and of limited value to the student. Be careful not to let workbooks or workbook exercises substitute for teaching.

If you do not have enough books to cut up, use transparent material, such as tracing paper, onion skin paper, or a sheet of clear acetate, to cover the page you wish to use; have the student write his answers on the transparent material, so that the book remains clean. (If you use clear plastic sheets, the student can write on them with crayon that can be wiped off.)

7. An excellent means of encouraging self-expression is to dramatize different situations. **Role-playing** is an interesting and effective activity for all age groups. Although it may be more exciting when done with groups of students, it can also be managed very nicely in individual instruction, with the tutor and the student acting, or role-playing together.

The telephone is a useful prop for dramatic self-expression. Many students have never handled a telephone, or have so little experience with the instrument that they become fearful in relation to it. These students should receive assistance in learning the mechanics of making a phone call. (The local telephone company will sometimes make sample instruments available to the tutor for use in such instruction.) Others will find it easier to speak into an instrument than to address a person directly. In both cases, self-expression is encouraged through the use of the phone.

Other situations and relationships that may be dramatized are those of parent and child, teacher and student, the job interview, shopping for a particular item, how to travel, and an interview at a social or welfare agency.

The use of hand puppets in role-playing with children adds variety and color to the drama. Inexpensive puppets may be purchased, or they may be made at the tutoring session by drawing on paper bags and by crayoning or inking with a felt-tipped pen on old white socks.

8. A **typewriter and a tape recorder** are helpful in reading instruction. They may be used to stimulate interest and to add variety to the lesson. You may have the student type stories; at other time, you may type his stories. The tape recorder may be used to record progress in oral reading or to record discussions and stories; the student learns a good deal by listening to himself, and usually enjoys it.

9. **Games** are fun, and fun should be part of the learning experience. Games take time, and you are impatient for the learning to take place quickly. But it also takes time to learn in an area in which one has experienced failure. Games provide opportunities for success—in knowing an answer so that one gets the next move—and, sometimes, in winning the game. Games are useful also because they take the monotony and drudgery out of practice, which the student needs and from which s/he benefits.

In games of skill, you will more often be the winner at the beginning. In games of chance, where the moves depend on a spinner or the roll of dice, players have equal chances of winning. Even though the student is eager to win, and you would like the student to win, play fairly and do not give the student a false sense of winning; s/he will know that you yielded; it will not help his self-esteem. It is best to avoid competitive games; adapt the games of skill so that each player tries to beat his last score, thus competing with himself rather than with the other players.

The best games are often home-made, though there are many useful commercial games. See page 209 for a list of game manufacturers.

10. The **computer, the television set, and the VCR** may not be available to you in the tutorial program, but it is important for you to know the good and bad features of each, and how they may be helpful in the program, if they are available.

Television and VCR

Your students are exposed to Television and VCR for many hours each week. It is not necessary for you to introduce them into your sessions with the student. It is important nevertheless to be realistic about your student's exposure to these media. They can serve as a basis for discussion; the student may describe his favorite program:

- he may describe the sequence of events: what happened and when
- Why was it interesting?
- What was important?
- Why did the protagonist do what s/he did?
- What were his alternatives?
- Why did the student like or dislike the program?

In other words, discussion of these programs can help develop analytical and critical thinking skills far beyond the level at which the student is able to read.

The Computer

If your program has a computer, and has computer game or instructional programs, they may or may not be helpful with your students.

Before you use a computer game (or program) with your student, try it yourself.

In your judgment, do you have all the equipment required for this game: a joystick? a mouse? a color monitor?

Is the program at the right level for your student? Does it provide a challenge? Is the challenge not too great to be frustrating?

Is the program too speedy? Is it too slow?

Does it give feedback on correct answers and errors?

For companies that publish computer programs, see pages 210-211.

CONCLUSION

You will have failures; you may be discouraged by lack of progress; you may feel that you have been unable to make contact with your student; you may feel discomfort with a particular student.

All of these problems arise with the best of teachers and with the most experienced. That they arise does not necessarily reflect on you; ask your supervisor for advice on how to deal with them. At times, you will want to request an evaluation of a special student by other specialists if you are working in a team setting where a counselor, a psychologist, or a psychiatrist is available.

In those cases in which you feel you have not made contact with a particular student, or feel uncomfortable with him, it is your privilege to request that s/he be transferred to another tutor. Other students will in turn come to you from other tutors.

Concern about failures and lack of progress is the daily lot of the good teacher; should you feel such concern, your supervisor will assist you with new materials and techniques, if that is necessary, or with reassurance, if that is all that is called for.

Working with School Children

1. Because the experience and vocabulary of children is limited, trips are very important. Take the children to a pet shop, zoo or animal farm, museum, library, fire house.

2. Associate reading with pleasure for them; read to them for a few minutes each day. Play-act the story with them; this will help encourage self-expression.

3. Use games as part of the instruction. In enjoying the game, children learn their reading skills at the same time. Do not feel impatient because the games take so long to play. The pleasure associated with the instructional time and the satisfaction derived from every correct move made in the game are positive gains for the child.

4. Spend time having fun with words. This gives the child practice in listening to the sounds of words, an important skill in learning to read. Make rhymes. Read nonsense poems. Play games naming things that start with the same sounds or letters, like " 'A"—my name is Alice and my husband's name is Allan; we come from Alabama and we live on Amity Street." Play GEOGRAPHY.
Many children have difficulties with language. They have not yet learned to understand words of relationship, abstract words and concepts, colloquial expressions and idioms. See lists on page 67 for sample words and expressions that often require explanation.

5. Avoid using the same textbook and workbook for tutoring that the child is using in his classroom at school.

6. Do not assume that the child is at the reading level expected at his age—or in his grade—or even that s/he is at the reading level of the reading text that s/he uses at school. Many children are given readers in school that are in fact beyond their reading levels. You will have to evaluate the child's reading level yourself; see page 86.

7. It may be helpful, where possible, to meet with the child's classroom teacher to discuss common goals and to indicate to the teacher that the child is expending additional effort outside of school. Before

doing this, however, discuss the idea with your supervisor; in some cases, s/he may consider the meeting inappropriate or impractical.

8. If the child comes to you directly after school, ascertain whether your project is able to provide milk and cookies, or some other light snack for the child. Hunger will interfere with his learning.

9. To help form positive associations with the learning experience, some token rewards are useful during the early stages of remedial instruction. These may be small items costing no more than a few cents, such as a ball, a set of jacks, rubber stamps, a book or some marbles; stars, which are traditional tokens of reward, are also encouraging and helpful with some children. These should not be viewed as bribes, but rather as incentive rewards. As the instruction progresses, the need for these incentives disappears; learning will then be its own reward. On occasion children will ask for "presents" even when they have not been earned. The tutor must explain simply and clearly that the prizes are rewards and are given only when earned; when the tutor is consistent, firm and pleasant, children will accept the rules graciously.

The cost of these rewards, as that of the snack mentioned earlier, should be borne by the program, not the tutor. Frequently, cooperative community organizations and friendly businessmen will contribute or help defray their cost when they are made aware of the need.

10. Many children cannot stay put with one task for very long. For this reason, it is very important to prepare many different activities for the one session; before the child wearies of one activity, it is wise to shift to another. It is helpful at times to introduce some opportunity for the child to move around: to get a drink of water or to play *Simple Simon* for a few minutes before returning to a new table activity.

11. Some children who present behavior problems at school will try to "test" the tutor while they are getting to know him . They want to know just what the rules are, just what they can get away with, and what the tutor will not tolerate. They may come late, or come on time but refuse to do the work, or try to shock the tutor with their language. Such behavior is best handled without reproach, but with gentle and firm reminders of what is acceptable to the tutor and what the rules are. If the child is not ready to settle down for the session, it may be hepful to suspend formal instruction for the day with a reminder that you will plan to teach him the content at the next session when s/he is ready

to work. Review your plan for the day to be sure that the activities are varied enough to assist in capturing the child's attention and cooperation more completely next time.

Working with School Dropouts and Adults

1. Although dropouts have failed academically and may consider themselves stupid, they are frequently desperately anxious to learn some of what they missed. Some were certain that they could succeed in the outside world, when they dropped out of school. They did try; they found the experience bitter. Jobs are difficult to get, and even dead-end jobs are demanding. The employer wants them on the job on time, dressed properly, and the pay may be small. The work may be boring, and sometimes seems to be menial. Most of the time dropouts are unemployed, and unhappy about this. They come to your agency for some service—possibly for a job; and someone has persuaded them to try once more to learn some "schoolwork." In a sense, they are challenging your program: "No teacher was ever able to teach me before. Do you think you are any better?"

You will have to rise to this challenge. Until now, no one has given them so much individual attention; no one has set for them small goals, which are in effect promises, and then kept those promises. With gentle, firm reassurance, you can build their self-confidence and help them to learn.

2. Some of your students come involuntarily: they are required to attend a remedial program in order to meet the requirements of some program in which they are involved. In some cases, they are penalized if they do not attend; funds for their support are reduced. Sometimes they receive a stipend for attending a remedial program. These students present a great challenge: your goal is to motivate them to want to learn, without regard for the money associated with attending the program. Learning requires more than attendance: it requires interest, motivation, confidence that one can learn, and confidence that it is worthwhile to invest effort in learning.

3. If they are beginning readers, work slowly and patiently. Be sure to seek out or create materials of interest to adults. If you have to use material designed for children, adults will usually accept them if you explain that unfortunately this is all that is available, and that, since materials are only a tool, even these materials can be helpful. As soon as possible, bring in the adult material.

4. With this group, the caution stated earlier about privacy is essential. Never permit these older students to be taught where younger children may observe them. Also, it may be embarrassing to your student to carry books that are obviously at a low reading level; cover his books with a college book jacket.

5. As soon as the student is ready for supplementary independent reading, lend him a book to read. All of his life s/he may have wanted to carry a book that s/he could read, just as other people do.

6. If the reading grade level of your student is between the fourth and ninth grades, relate the reading instruction to vocational goals. For example, if a young man is interested in being an auto mechanic, find manuals, instruction guides, and books about cars and mechanics to arouse and maintain his interest.

7. If the reading level is at the ninth grade or higher, set the goal of achieving the G.E.D., or high school equivalency certificate. Call the local high school for information about the examination for this certificate. Plan your instruction in relation to the examination requirements. The certificate has prestige as well as vocational and college-entrance value. It is an important goal.

8. Avoid references to school grades and to levels of ability. Have each student compete with his own record, not with that of other students.

9. Remember that adults have a wide range of experience and a relatively full vocabulary, though they may be illiterate.

10. Avoid condescension in your tone, in your language, and in the materials and subject matter you select.

11. Discussion, brain-storming, newspapers, organization: You have much to learn from drop-outs and adults who are intelligent and

well-informed in many ares in which you may be ignorant. Discussions and "brain-storming" in areas of mutual interest (current events, community problems, etc.) are invaluable adjuncts of reading instruction in encouraging oral expression, sharpening thinking skills, and building self-confidence.

12. Adults who have never had the opportunity to learn to read have not been school failures; therefore they may not have suffered as much damage to their self-esteem as have dropouts. Their self-esteem is wanting, nevertheless, because they are aware of their great handicap in daily life and in vocational competence. They, too, fear failure; they suspect that they are "too dumb" or too old to learn anything. Adults will be responsive to instruction, provided that they are treated with utmost courtesy and respect, with praise for every achievement, and with no reproaches. Adults can discipline themselves to stick to a job and to work hard at it, if they see results. They will do homework if they feel they are learning something useful.

Part **2**

Working With Students for Whom English Is a Foreign Language

LEARNING ABOUT THE STUDENT'S WORLD

The number of non-English-speaking children and adults in our schools is large. Since English is a foreign language for them, their problems in learning it are quite special. Because the student must learn to speak a second language before or while s/he learns to read it, and is at the same time adjusting to a new way of life, it is harder for him to remain interested in his work. The teacher or tutor requires an unusual background of information, understanding and sensitivity in order to assist the non-English-speaking student to learn.

You will have to know a good deal about the world of the student, and how it contrasts with your own. You will be unable to fully understand the student's behavior and his responses unless you know about his culture and values—his habits and routines, his family ties, what behaviors are considered proper and commendable, and those that are considered bad or even unimportant.

Cultural differences have made this country vital and dynamic. You should therefore accept and tolerate these cultural and value differences, though you may feel very keenly and with great conviction about your own background and values. You must understand that your student grew and developed his behavior patterns in a different environment from your own, and was surrounded by different cultural practices. Now that the student has been transplanted into what is, for him, a strange world, his values may change, as may yours as well. But these changes must be a natural result of the exchange between student and tutor. The tutor may not sit in judgment of the student's world. The differences must be accepted and tolerated, and through them, you, the tutor, can indeed gain insights into the student and his behavior through your growing knowledge of his culture.

Let us examine several cultural patterns that may differ. Though these illustrations will probably not relate to any one of your students, they demonstrate how important it is to reserve judgment when the student's behavior is somewhat disconcerting or distressing. Upon further study, you may find that such behavior can be completely rational when viewed in the context of the student's cultural background.

The following illustrations may make the contrasts more clear:

1. Punctuality is very important in mainstream American industrialized society. In warmer climates, with less seasonal contrasts in temperature, and in places where there is little industry, people have tended to have less regard for punctuality than have those in our highly

mechanized society. Though it may be inconvenient when a student is late for an appointment, the tutor must recognize that this apparently cavalier attitude towards punctuality may be part of a cultural pattern, and is not intended to be a personal affront.

2. Sex roles in many countries are often more sharply contrasted than in the United States. Quite often the male is the absolute head of the group. He makes decisions while the female is usually more passive. The man earns the living for the family; the woman takes care of the home. In preparation for the adult roles, the child's play anticipates the expected adult behavior: boys must not play sissy games; girls may not play rough games. Although these patterns are changing, the cultural contrasts in sex roles remain striking.

3. In some cultures, cooperation has received greater stress than has competition. When students who have been taught cooperation as a way of life take examinations, it might seem natural for them to share their answers freely. In a competitive society, such sharing is frowned upon, and is called "cheating." This behavior (the sharing of answers on tests) must be seen as the result of a cooperative background, rather than as a sign of dishonesty). If the student is to succeed, or even survive, in a competitive society, it may be that s/he will have to be taught to compete.

The importance of accepting and understanding cultural and language differences cannot be stressed enough, for as a result of these differences, many children of minority groups have poor self-esteem, are embarrassed about the contrast between language spoken at home and that at school, and puzzled about the contrast between behavior expected at home and at school (those we call cultural differences). Their language problems frequently contribute to their school failures, compounding their lack of self-esteem. The sensitive teacher, the sensitive tutor, can counteract this feeling of inadequacy, and can help pave the way to success for the student. The finest proof of the tutor's respect for the culture of the student is the tutor's ability to converse with the student in his native language; this skill is invaluable. The tutor who lacks this knowledge can show respect by learning some common words and phrases from the student. This provides a double benefit: the tutor acquires a smattering of a second language and at the same time forms a bond with the student.

As mentioned above, language is a central feature in the culture of any group. The student who feels isolated in an unfriendly English speaking world, surrounded by people who look down at those s/he loves, may feel more comfortable, wanted and loved, speaking only his native language with his own group. He may fail to learn to speak English for these reasons.

You must demonstrate in your behavior and in your speech that you respect your students, that you respect their background and culture, that they are worthy individuals, and that you have confidence in their ability to learn.

Motivation, Self-Esteem

Basic to the student's learning, and as an accompaniment to the instruction, is a continuing sense of unity with his native world, even while entering the new English-speaking world. Pride in self can be strengthened while learning through the use of materials based on the culture and background of the student. Your neighborhood librarian will help you locate such materials. Look for biographies of heroes of his culture; your student will enjoy these, take pride in them, and maintain his interest in learning.

Remember that, as for all students, motivation and instruction must focus on materials that will be of interest to a student of his age, and teach him those skills that s/he lacks. Keep in mind that there is no one best way for all students in all situations. Find the best way for your student.

Specific Language Problems

Non-English-speaking students arrive in this country at any time of the year. Therefore, they may be admitted to school and placed in classes in which the students already know each other, know school routines, and have participated in a certain amount of group learning. The new arrival is a stranger to all of these, and must adjust to the other students, to the routines, and to the curriculum all at the same time. The new student is usually placed in the class appropriate for his age, and thus, s/he will be with other students of his age. Yet some of these new students may have had very little schooling previously. They may come from areas in which educational opportunities were limited, or they may come from the families of migrant workers so that their schooling has been repeatedly interrupted. Their native tongue may be Spanish, Navajo, Turkish, Italian, Russian, or an Asian language, such as Chinese. Some understand no English at all, while others may understand much of what they hear, may speak haltingly, and yet may be unable to read. Some live in communities where only their native language is spoken, and English is regarded as a strange tongue. They may be of all ages: school children, adolescents, adults, or old people. Even among those who have had previous instruction in English, there has been no uniform curriculum; each student, therefore, knows different things.

For young children, learning a second language can be as easy as learning a first language; they learn spontaneously from the language of everyday life. Yet teaching English as a second language in school, where English is the only language spoken, is not as successful. Children in school who do not speak English are unable at the same time to learn to read, to learn arithmetic, and all other subjects requiring the English language—thus compounding their failure.

Learning English: Speaking and Listening

Before non-English-speaking students can be taught to read English, they must acquire some listening and speaking skills. The first phase of instruction therefore must concentrate on the acquisition of oral language skills; these include the development of vocabulary and the ability to hold a conversation.

Some students understand spoken English quite well, but are self-conscious about expressing themselves. They must be encouraged to speak, with corrections limited to major rather than trivial errors. Although your area of responsibility is reading, with this group of students you may have to expand it to include speech.

The student must be encouraged to talk and write and read about himself, his home, his culture, his community, his interests, his wishes, needs and emotions. To maintain interest and to encourage communication, simple but real conversations should be encouraged from the first day. The meaning should always be clear to the student; the student should never be asked to repeat, to read or to practice material whose meaning is not clear to him. He should be led to understand the material, by relating it, whenever possible, to his own experience. As his speech develops, s/he will be ready for reading and writing more quickly. He will thus also be ready to participate in the total learning program more readily.

Oral practice of new words, phrases, and sentences is essential. Natural conversation is one way of giving the student practice. He is thus able to repeat what s/he has heard. Good pronunciation is learned most easily by imitation of the tutor or another English-speaking person. If the student has difficulty in imitating, or speaks with a heavy accent, remember that your goal is that s/he speak understandably, not perfectly. If you can understand him, his speech is adequate. Try to limit the number of corrections that you make; you do not want the student to feel unsuccessful. Praise him when you can understand him, and whenever s/he has overcome an obstacle.

Sometimes a student will have special difficulty with a particular sound: s/he may say **sheep** for **ship** or **pin** for **pen**. If his accent or dialect (when s/he substitutes these sounds) makes it difficult to understand him, you may want to give him practice in saying these sounds correctly. In that case, always practice the sounds as part of words; do not have him practice the sounds in isolation as they lose all meaning for the student in this way.

Some English words and phrases, when pronounced with a foreign accent, sound quite different, and seem to mean something different, thus causing confusion to the listener, and embarrassment to the speaker. For example:

under	may sound like	*on the*
hat	may sound like	*hot*
it	may sound like	*eat*
day	may sound like	*they*
bleed	may sound like	*breathe*

The learner who finds himself repeatedly misunderstood may retreat to his own language, and give up his attempts to learn to read and speak English.

Many foreign languages omit personal pronouns, or use them in simplified form. Our pronouns, particularly **he**, **she**, **his** and **her**, are therefore very difficult for many to learn correctly.

Children under twelve will learn to speak without an accent more easily than will older learners. If you are teaching a young child, therefore, be confident that your conversations with him in English, and his conversations and play with English-speaking children of his age at school and in the community, and even his listening to the radio and television, all will contribute to his learning to speak English well and without an accent. Remember never to criticize an accent, or a dialect, because you will then be criticizing the child's family and his community in which s/he is surrounded by accents. When correcting the student, concentrate only on a specific pronunciation, a specific sound used in different words.

In order to be able to speak the language well, the student must have good listening skills. He must be able to hear all the correct sounds, words, and word groups, and understand them in the general context. If s/he misses the meaning of a word because s/he misheard one of the sounds, or because he does not understand the word, he will then lose much of the material that follows. The tutor must speak and work at the speed most comfortable for the student so that this problem can be avoided. The student must also be able to remember what he heard at the beginning, and throughout the listening period until the end, so that he may have a grasp of the total meaning of the speaker. Conversation helps build listening skills, as does reading to the student material of interest to him.

Learning Written English: Reading and Writing

When your student has learned enough of the English language from school and through contact with you to be able to hold simple conversations with you, s/he is ready to begin to learn to read English. If s/he already knows how to read his native language, s/he will learn to read English quickly. In any case, teach him to read—following the guidelines in this manual. Find out what s/he knows, and, in a systematic way, teach those skills that s/he lacks. Be patient, be confident, and keep in mind that s/he has special problems and obstacles to overcome. Provide him with the opportunity for success and pride in his achievement, and both you and s/he will be rewarded by the progress that you will see.

As you already know, it is difficult to read English because it is not consistent in its spelling. Thus, after learning how to sound out, the reader must learn a great many exceptions to the usual rules.

A single letter may represent several different sounds, as does the **o** in each of the following words:

Tom, hole, of

The letters ea sound quite different in each of these words:

beans, bear, heart

Despite all of the difficulties enumerated, your student can and will learn if you have confidence that s/he will learn, and if you follow the guidelines outlined in this book.

Words that are Similar in English and Spanish

Spanish and English have many words in common. Following are some of the similarities that have been observed*, between Spanish and English, together with illustrations. You can make similar comparisons of English with the native language of any of your students.

1. Some words are exactly the same in English and Spanish. This happens most often with words that end in **or**, **al**, and **able**.

decimal	general
continental	conductor
formidable	considerable

2. Some words in Spanish are the same as their English equivalents, except that in Spanish they have a final vowel, **a**, **e**, or **o**.

Spanish	English
aparente	apparent
cosmetico	cosmetic
forma	form
idiota	idiot
inconveniente	inconvenient

3. Words ending in **cion** in Spanish end in **tion** in English.

Spanish	English
donacion	donation
determinaction	determination
graduacion	graduation
mocion	motion
ocupacion	occupartion

---

*"Vocabulary Guide of Cognate Words in Spanish and English," Stanley Krippner, Maimonedes Hospital of Brooklyn, New York, 1966

4. Some words in Spanish can be changed to English by doubling the first, second or last consonant of the word.

ilegal	illegal
mision	mission
mocasin	moccasin

5. Some Spanish words can be changed to English by changing the final letter **a** or **o** in Spanish to **e** in English.

defensia	defense
delicado	delicate
globo	globe
impulso	impulse
medicina	medicine

6. Some Spanish words can be changed to English by changing the final **ia** or **io** in Spanish to **y** in English.

diario	diary
geometria	geometry
infancia	infancy
memoria	memory
onopolio	monopoly

7. Some Spanish words can be changed to English by changing the letters **c** or **t** in Spanish to **ch** and **th** in English.

eter	ether
autor	author
catederal	cathedral
caracter	character
coral	choral

8. In some words, change the Spanish **cia** or **cio** to **ce** in English.

palacio	palace
presencia	presence
servicio	service
silencio	silence
distancia	distance

9. In some words, change the final **fia** or **phia** in Spanish to **phy** in English.

bibliographia	bibliography
opografia	topography
caligrafia	calligraphy

10. In some words, change the final letters **dad** in Spanish to **ty** in English.

varaedad	variety
volocidad	velocity
vitalidad	vitality
oportunidad	opportunity
capacidad	capacity
calridad	clarity

Words and Phrases that Confuse the Non-English-Speaking Learner

Vocabulary may be divided into **content words** and **function words**. **Content words** are those we can see, touch, illustrate. They are names of things (nouns), action words (verbs), and words that describe nouns and verbs (adjectives and adverbs).

Function words are the connecting and other words which have little concrete meaning in themselves, but which make it possible to get the total meaning out of statements. These are prepositions, auxiliaries and conjunctions, such as **and**, **on**, **to**, **the**, **by**, **for**, **but**.

Look at this sentence:

The *big brown fox jumped* over the *beautiful table*.

The content words are in italics. Content words are easier to teach and easier to learn when they are very concrete and related to the experience of the learner. The content words in the above sentence are easy to illustrate and easy to explain to the learner.

Consider this sentence:

John is very *loyal* and *honest*.

In this sentence, the content words **loyal** and **honest** are abstract: they are difficult to visualize and difficult to explain. Reserve the abstract words until your student is able to converse with you in a relaxed way, and has acquired a useful concrete vocabulary.

When you teach the non English-speaking student, begin by teaching those words that are easiest to illustrate and to visualize, or even to touch, to handle, and to smell. As you set these words into sentences, in your conversations with the student, the function words, (the, and, but, of, how) are presented to him naturally. Although these words are more difficult to learn, they will become part of his vocabulary as s/he learns to converse with you.

Point to objects in the room and name them. Name objects in magazines and in books. Prepare a grab bag of objects; have the student reach in, take them out one at a time, and name them.

You may converse with your student about many things in English: school, his favorite game, how s/he likes his work, television.

Common expressions, such as **goodbye**, **hello**, **how are you**, **so**, **well**, must be taught to the student systematically so that s/he may understand them and also use them.

Idiomatic expressions can be very confusing to the non English speaking student. So can words with several meanings.

The student will have difficulty understanding these sentences:

His head was spinning.

He hit the nail on the head.

Such idioms are usually translated literally and immediately lose all meaning. The foreign speaker is confused by a word that has several meanings or by words that sound the same; s/he sometimes selects the inappropriate priate meaning and loses the sense of the conversation. For Example:

The king reigned (rained ?) for 20 years.

Compound words often have meanings that are astonishing to the foreign ear. On pages 71, 182 are some of the words and phrases that require special attention, if your student is to understand spoken English. You will think of many more examples.

At the beginning, be careful not to use contractions. Say **I do not** rather than **I don't**; **will not**, rather than **won't**. After s/he is able to converse comfortably, s/he will be able to learn the contractions more easily. On page 75 are some of the common phrases, expressions and categories that are helpful to the student who is learning to speak English.

Some Spanish speaking students tend to drop their final **s** sounds. This is a common practice in Puerto Rico, and sometimes the habit is carried over to the English language. Look upon this as part of an old habit, rather than an error. Eventually the student will learn to retain the final **s**.

The English language has a debt to many other languages; although it is basically of Anglo-Saxon origin, it has borrowed manywords from Latin. It has many words in common with many of the native languages spoken by your students. In addition, many languages have recently borrowed English words and made part of their own languages. For example, in French, we find the word **rosbif** (roast beef).

Remember that all of us understand much more of the language than we can use; your student will recognize and understand more words than s/he is able to incorporate into his own speaking vocabulary.

WORDS THAT SOUND SIMILIAR

slick	but	except	gorilla	reel	son
sleek	butt	accept	guerilla	real	sun
sink	ball	fair	hear	right	stair
zinc	bell	fare	here	write	stare
quit	be	rain	hole	rode	there
quite	bee	reign	whole	road	their
ever	by	sew	holy	sail	to
every	buy	so	wholly	sale	too
					two
umpire	bin	knew	seam		
empire	been	new	seem	waist	
				waste	
trial	berry	know	sea		
trail	bury	no	see		
which	close	lesson			
witch	clothes	lessen	seen		
			scene		
eminent	desert	meat			
imminent	dessert	meet			
			sell		
		miner	cell		
weather	die	minor			
whether	dye		sent		
		plain	cent		
affect	do	plane	scent		
effect	dew				
trial	berry	know	sea		
trail	bury	no	see		

Guidelines to Teaching Remedial Reading

COMPOUND WORDS

(See page 182 for more compound words.)

sawbones	browbeat	farfetched	shorthand
headshrinker	aboveboard	firsthand	shorthanded
sourpuss	beeline	bandwagon	highbrow
knothead	skyscraper	halfhearted	lowbrow
screwball	breakdown	holdover	handout
windbag	checkup	layoff	bottleneck
hothead	dropout	makeup	blackout
greenhorn			

SELECTED LIST OF IDIOMS that Confuse Many Students with Reading Problems, as Well as Those Who Are Learning English as a Foreign Language*

A-1	At first blush
Of age	At least
All at once	At one's fingertips
All ears	At one's wits' end
All in	At the top
All in all	Ax to grind
All right	Back number
Apple of one's eye	Back on his feet
Apple-pie order	Back out
As a matter of fact	Back up
As yet	Bad blood
At fault	Bad egg

*Dictonary of Idioms, Lillie Pope, in preparation, Book Lab, New York

Bag and baggage

Beard the lion

Beat about the bush

Behind one's back

Below the belt

Beside oneself

Beside the point

Better half

Between the devil and the deep sea

Big hand

Big shot

Birds of a feather

Bite one's head off

Blind date

Blow off steam

Bone to pick

Bosom friends

Break away

Break the ice

Bring home the bacon

Bring to mind

Brush-off

Burn the candle at both ends

Close call

Cock and bull story

Come in handy

Cook one's goose

Cool as a cucumber

Count one's chickens before they are hatched

Crack a joke

Burst into tears

Bury the hatchet

Butt in

By and large

By the skin of one's teeth

By the way

Call up

Carry on

Carry the ball

Catch fire

Catch one's eye

Catch red-handed

Chain smoker

Chalk up

Change hands

Change one's mind

Check in

Check out

Chew the fat

Chin up

Chips are down

Eat one's heart out

Eat one's words

Elbow grease

Face the music

Fair and square

Fall apart

Cream of the crop

Cry wolf

Dark horse

Dead as a doornail

Dirty look

Do away with

Dog-tired

Doll up

Double-cross

Down to earth

Draw the line

Drop by (drop in)

Drop in the bucket

Drop off

Dutch treat

Eat one's cake and have it too

From A to Z

Get even with

Get in one's hair

Get in touch with

Get it off your chest

Get on one's nerves

Get the upper hand

Get under one's skin

Get wind of

Ghost of a chance

Give a piece of one's mind

Give in

Give the cold shoulder

Go-getter

Far cry

Farfetched

Feather in one's cap

Feather one's nest

Feel blue

Feel it in one's bones

Fence sitter

Fifty-fifty

Finger in every pot (in every pie)

Fit as a fiddle

Flash in the pan

Fly in the ointment

Fool around

Foot the bill

For a song

Forty winks

Have a lot on the ball

Have a screw loose

Have cold feet

Have irons in the fire

Have one's hands full

Have one's heart in one's mouth

Head over heels

Hold back

Hold one's horses

Hold one's tongue

Holding the bag

Hot air

In a nutshell

In clover

Go out of one's way | In dutch

Go straight | In one's right mind

Go to bat for | In the doghouse

Go to pot | In the nick of time

Half-baked | Jot down

Halfhearted | Jump at

Hand-to-mouth | Keep house

Handle with kid gloves | Keep in touch with

Have a bone to pick | Keep one's head

Keep the wolf from the door | Nose to the grindstone

Kill two birds with one stone | Old hand

Know the ropes | On its last legs

Ladies' man | On the dot

Laugh up one's sleeve | On the whole

Lay off | Out of the question

Leave no stone unturned | Pay through the nose

Left-handed compliment | Play the market

Leg to stand on | Play with fire

Lend an ear | Pull a boner

Like a fish out of water | Pull one's leg

Look down on | Put one's foot down

Lose one's shirt | Put one's foot in one's mouth

Make a clean breast | Put two and two together

Make a mountain out of a molehill

Make believe | Queer duck

Make ends meet | Raw deal

Make eyes at | Right-hand man

Make no bones about | Rub someone the wrong way

Make one's blood boil | Run across

Meet halfway

Monkey around with

Nip in the bud

See eye to eye

Skate on thin ice

Slip through one's fingers

Smell a rat

Sneeze at

Split hairs

Step on the gas

Stick one's neck out

Stiff upper lip

Straight from the horse's mouth

Straight from the shoulder

Stretch a point

Strike while the iron is hot

Stuffed shirt

Take the bull by the horns

Save face

Say a mouthful

Scare the daylights out of

Talk shop

Talk through his hat

Talk turkey

Through thick and thin

Throw in the sponge

To be of age

Tom, Dick and Harry

Tongue lashing

Turn over a new leaf

Under the weather

Under his thumb

Upset the applecart

White elephant

Win hands down (thumbs down)

COMMON PHRASES, EXPRESSIONS AND CATEGORIES That Are Helpful For Those Whom English Is A Second Language

My name is ——.

I live at——.

I go to school at ——-.

I am in the — grade.

My teacher is ——.

My telephone number is ——-.

I am thirsty (hungry.)

I do not understand.

Please speak more slowly.

Please repeat.

I do not feel well.

My mother is sick.

I was late because ———.

I was absent because ———.

I must go to the bathroom.

Can we play this game?

Can we read this?

Today is Monday.

How are you?

I am fine, thank you.

Where is ———?

How much is ———?

I am very sorry.

Good morning, sir (miss, madam).

Good afternoon (evening).

Good bye.

I want to eat lunch.

I want a drink of water.

I would like a glass of milk.

The line is busy.

There is no answer.

Who is speaking?

This is ——— talking.

You have the wrong number.

To whom do you wish to speak?

I wish to speak to ———.

I am cold (hot).

Yes

No

Please

Where

Hello

Good-bye

Thank you

Excuse me

Where is ———?

I like cake (bread, milk, fruit, egg).

Where is the toilet (bathroom)?

It is there? It is here?

What is your name?

What is your address?

Where do you live?

Which bus (train) goes to ———?

Did you eat breakfast (lunch, dinner)?

Are you hungry?

What time is it? What time do you have?

It is nine o'clock.

What time does the bus leave?

It is early (late, very early, very late).

Yesterday (today, tomorrow)

Last night

This afternoon

This morning

What day is today?

Today is November 15.

Today is a beautiful day.

It is hot (cold, cloudy, raining, sunny, windy).

What will be the weather tomorrow?

The sun is shining today.

CATEGORIES

Numbers

Colors

Clothes

Parts of the body

Days of the week

Months of the year

Furniture

Food

Coins

Persons, such as **girl**, **boy, man, woman, child**

Family relationships, such as **daughter, grandmother, sister**

See pages 182, 192-5 for additional compound words, figurative language, idioms and other words that are difficult for many people to understand, and certainly are difficult for students for whom English is a foreign language.

Part 3

How To Teach

What You Need to Know About Reading

The ability to read requires the simultaneous use of many skills. At its most primitive level, it requires the ability to understand the meaning of the printed symbol. In order to understand, it is at the same time necessary to decode the printed words. Thus, it is not sufficient to be able to recite the printed words, as, for example: *Both fission and fusion were involved in the hydrogen bomb.* Reading this sentence requires that one understand it as well.

On a simpler level, in order to read the sentence **Tom is fat**, the reader must know:
- that English is read from left to right;
- how to sound the consonants **t, m, f**;
- how to sound the short vowels **o, a**;
- how to blend consecutive sounds in words to make a smooth-sounding word: **f a t** to sound **fat**;
- how to recognize **is** at sight;
- that **Tom** is a proper name;
- the meaning of the word **fat**.

As the reader becomes proficient at decoding and understanding the literal meaning of the printed word, it is hoped that her understanding (comprehension) becomes three-dimensional: that s/he feels comfortable enough with the written matter so that s/he may read into it, analyze it, and ask critical questions about the meaning. At an advanced level, therefore, the reading process expands to include many of the thought processes that are helpful in meeting and coping with the demands of life. Reading then becomes a source of information and pleasure throughout life.

This is our goal in facilitating learning how to read. Many learn to read spontaneously, easily and happily from repeated exposure to books, and with excellent instruction in the schools. Unfortunately, some fail to learn to read. Learners who have already stumbled and fallen, emergent illiterates, require special instruction geared to undoing the harm that has been caused by their repeated failures.

Writing is closely tied to reading skills. In order to develop and advance reading skills, and to encourage expressive language, the reader should be encouraged at *every* level to express himself in writing: keep a log or a diary, write about an incident or a worry, tell a story.

Comprehension skills and writing will be discussed in greater detail on pages 123, 127, 131. It is important at this time, however, that you understand these dimensions of the process of reading.

LITERACY

Many of the students in remedial programs are labeled illiterate. There are those who are:

Completely Illiterate Persons who can read none or only a few words may be called *illiterate*. Their knowledge of reading is so inadequate that it is useless in most life situations.

Functionally Illiterate is the term sometimes applied to those whose reading achievement is at the fourth grade level or below. They may read sufficiently well to be able to travel—that is, they can read signs, or simple instructions—and read an illustrated tabloid newspaper. But their reading ability is inadequate for vocational competence in any work involving more than the simplest reading. Such people cannot read instructions for assembling or repairing equipment; they cannot read contracts that they are called up to sign, nor can they read for pleasure. Moreover, they cannot read well enough to acquire the information that is essential for every responsible citizen. Such people may easily be limited to dead-end jobs in the lowest economic rung of the job ladder.

GRADE LEVELS

In the instructional situation, reading is often spoken of in terms of grade level. Grade levels in reading materials refer to relative difficulty of the material and to the school grade in which a child is usually expected to be able to read that material. The number of words in a sentence, the number of syllables in the words, and the content all contribute to the determination of grade levels in reading matter. For example, children in the third grade are expected to read at the third grade level. A level of 3.2 means the second month of the third grade. Usually, children in the third grade are eight years old; the exceptions are those who have been held over, or accelerated, or who entered school late for special reasons. As reading skill increases, the reader is able to read more involved material and can absorb concepts of greater complexity.

A student's reading grade level as ascertained by testing is not necessarily an accurate indication of her true reading ability since her score may be influenced by the way s/he is tested, as well as by any of several external factors. (To better understand reading levels and the skills they reflect, you might ask your supervisor for a copy of a written reading test, which you can then administer to yourself and correct.) In general, a student's reading grade level is helpful to the teacher as a rough guide, before refining the diagnosis of her reading problem. To help you appreciate the significance of a given reading level, we will describe what is generally expected in each grade, though many surge forward more quickly, while some fall behind

.

Emergent Reader/Readiness for Formal Reading Instruction – (Kindergarten) – Usually Age 5

The student at this level can differentiate shapes; s/he knows some of the letters; s/he has been trained in left-to-right progression; s/he has become familiar with books, knows some of them very well, and, ideally, has pleasant associations with them.

Emergent Reader/Pre-Primer and Primer Level (First Grade) – Usually Age 6

The first grade student learns to recognize some words at sight; s/he learns to read some easy books, using the whole word and the whole language approach; s/he also learns to associate sounds with each of the consonants and with each of the short vowels. S/he acquires the ability to blend the sounds of a word as they appear consecutively, starting with the first sound at the left; s/he learns to do this smoothly, so that the word sounds natural when spoken.

Second Grade Level – Usually Age 7

The student in the second grade continues to read simple books in the classroom, while s/he learns more ways in which to analyze words. S/he learns the consonant blends (such as st and br).

Third Grade Level – Usually Age 8

At this level, the student's reading becomes smooth and fluent. "Reading" is no longer a goal in itself, but also becomes a tool for the acquisition of learning in other areas: history, geography, mythology, arithmetic, and fun.

Fourth Grade to Twelfth-Grade Level – Usually Ages 9 to 17

Beginning with fourth grade, and continuing upward, the emphasis in reading instruction continues to be on the acquisition of skill in attacking new words, increasing vocabulary, understanding what is read, and the improvement of study skills. At every grade level, the student's vocabulary—that is, the words s/he comprehends and speaks as well as those s/he reads—expands. At every grade level and at all times, s/he is also expected to derive pleasure from her reading.

ANOTHER WAY OF LOOKING AT READING LEVELS

1. **Instructional Reading Level**: This is the level at which the student should be taught. At this level, the student can

- read 95% of the words in the reading matter
- understand 75% of the material

2. **Independent Reading Level**: This is the highest level at which a person can read without assistance. It is usually one grade level below the instructional reading level. At this level, the student can

- read 99% of the words in the reading matter
- understand 90% or more of the material
- read smoothly and conversationally, and interpret the punctuation correctly.

3. **Frustration Level**: This is the lowest level at which the student is unable to deal with the reading matter. It is usually one grade level above the instructional reading level. At this level, the student

- reads less than 90% of the words
- understands less than 50% of the material
- struggles with many words
- is unable to read smoothly because of the massive effort needed to decode the words
- is FRUSTRATED.

4. **Aural Comprehension Level:** This is the level at which the student can understand material read to her. At this level, the student

- understands at least 75% of what is read to her
- discusses it at the same level as that of the selection, using vocabulary at that level, and providing information in the discussion from her own knowledge and experience.

How To Prepare A Reading Inventory

HOW TO FIND THE READING LEVEL

Use a series of graded readers. A graded reader is a school text that has a marking indicating the grade level for which it is intended. Select a sample of reading material near the end of each book in the series; each sample should be about 100 words long. Have your student read to you, beginning with the sample you are fairly confident s/he can read easily. If s/he misses **five words or less,** have her read to you a sample of the next (more difficult) reader. Continue in this way until s/he make **six or more errors in 100 words.**

The book in which s/he misses six or more words is too difficult for her; it marks her *Frustration Level.* The highest grade level in which s/he reads 95 or more words correctly out of 100 words is her *Instructional Level.* His *Independent Level*, at which s/he can read without assistance, is that in which s/he reads 98 of the vocabulary and understands at least 90% of the main ideas.

Many of your students will be unable to read fluently any of the texts in the series. Although they are in the higher grades, some may be able to read only a few letters of the alphabet and one or two words. Such students will be reading at the pre-primer level.

HOW TO EVALUATE COMPREHENSION

One must differentiate between general level of comprehension and level of reading comprehension. Students in remedial programs usually can understand spoken language at a far higher level than they can read. Reading comprehension refers to their understanding of the written word as they read it. The distinction between these two levels of comprehension is important.

To evaluate reading comprehension, have the student read silently a story from each book in the series. Have her answer questions about the main ideas, the vocabulary and the details. The book in which s/he answers correctly three-quarters of the questions is at her *instructional level*. If there is a discrepancy between the instructional grade level at which the student reads, and that at which s/he comprehends, the reading material presented to her should be at the lower level.

When her comprehension skill is greater than her reading skill (frequently the case with retarded readers), discussions should be at a more advanced level than that of her reading level. To evaluate the student's general level of comprehension, you may read to the student stories from books at higher levels, and then discuss each of the stories with her, searching for the main ideas, the details, and the vocabulary. When you have determined her oral comprehension level, it is important to converse with her at that level daily, and to discuss matters of interest and importance. In that way, you will supporting and advancing her relatively competent "thinking" skills, while at the same sessions you will help her to interpret the printed word.

WHEN THE STUDENT READS AT FOURTH GRADE LEVEL OR HIGHER

By the time s/he has learned to read at the fourth grade level, a student has usually learned to sound out unknown words, and therefore does not need much help in that area. If you discover some weakness or confusion in sounding out words, see the suggestions for dealing with this problem that appear on page 141 of this manual. Otherwise, material on how to teach the student who reads at the fourth grade level or higher can be found on pages 127 ff.

Concentrate on increasing her vocabulary, and on teaching her to analyze new words by breaking them down into syllables and by learning base words, prefixes, and suffixes. S/he must, in addition, learn study skills, so that s/he may use reading more efficiently as a tool in learning other subjects.

Needless to say, you will focus on comprehension skills as well. And s/he will be exposed to much literature so that s/he will learn from and love good books.

WHEN THE STUDENT READS AT THIRD GRADE LEVEL OR LOWER

Ascertain, by means of formal or informal evaluation procedures (see page 86), the answers to the following questions:

1. Is s/he able to read a selection?
2. Does s/he understand what s/he reads?
   a. Does s/he remember the details of what s/he has read?
   b. Does s/he understand the main idea?
   c. Does s/he see relationships: cause and effect, and similarities and differences?
   d. Does s/he understand the sequence and organization of what s/he has read?
   e. Is s/he able to draw inferences and conclusions from the reading matter?

or

3. Is s/he confused or inconsistent in following the printed line from left to right? Does s/he know her left from her right?
4. How many of the basic sight words does s/he know? Which words are unfamiliar to her?
5. What skills has s/he acquired in sounding out unknown words?
   a. Does s/he know the sounds of the consonants?
   b. Does s/he know the short vowel sounds?
   c. Does s/he know the long vowel sounds?
   d. Can s/he blend letter sounds easily to form words (**s a t** to **sat**)?
   e. Can s/he read the consonant blends (**st, br**)?
   f. Does s/he know the consonant combinations, (or digraphs) **ch, sh, th, wh**?
   g. Can s/he recognize vowel combinations, such as **oa, ai, ou ow**?
   h. Can s/he read vowels followed by **r** (**ar, er, ir, ur, or**)?

6. Is her inability to sound out words the result of her not having learned to discriminate between similar sounds when s/he hears them? For example, can s/he tell the difference between **lap** and **lack**, or **some** and **sun**? Note that students with foreign accents or dialects may have difficulty in saying the sounds as you do; this is not important. It is important that they learn to hear the differences in sounds, as an aid in word recognition.

The answers to the foregoing questions pinpoint your specific goals in teaching the student. An inventory* that is useful for evaluating some of the items just listed, particularly those relating to phonetic skills, follows. In all such attempts at evaluation, however, keep in mind that in day-to-day planning your observations are important and relevant. In addition to the specific reading skills to be observed and evaluated, the student's problems, interests, behavior patterns, work habits, patterns of speech, evidence of stammering or stuttering, motor coordination and general skills must be taken into account. The more the teacher understands these factors, the more effective the planning will be. In addition, the teacher's observation will be of interest to the supervisor or the specialist, if it becomes necessary to consult one.

Remember to chat with the student about her interests, vocational goals, recreation, and school experiences. In this way, you will become more aware of and better informed about your student's problems and needs and their relation to your program.

*Note that we try to avoid the use of the word **test**. It has unpleasant connotations for the student, implies pass or fail, and is not an accurate term for the teacher or tutor. The terms **evaluation** or **inventory**, on the other hand, denote a focus on the student's strengths, deficits, and interests with the view of amelioration, rather than on passing a harsh judgment on her competence.

Inventory of Basic Reading Skills*

This inventory will assist you in evaluating your student's strengths and weaknesses in beginning reading skills:

Name of Student_____

Date_____

Tutor_____

> *CAUTION: If your student makes five consecutive errors in any group of questions that follow, move on to the next group: when s/he has failed in the same way in three groups, stop testing. This inventory, and any other administered to students in remedial instruction, must be given with great sensitivity, and must minimize any feeling of failure, frustration, and pressure on the part of the student.*

I. Does s/he know left from right?

Ask these questions only if your student is under 12 years of age. List the responses in the appropriate column at the right.

	Correct	Hesitant	Incorrect
Point to your right eye.			
Point to your left eye.			
Which is your right hand?			
Point to your right ear.			
Point to your left eye.			
Which is your left hand?			

*Pope Inventory of Basic Reading Skills, Lillie Pope, New York, NY, Book Lab, 1974

II. How much sight vocabulary has s/he?

Some words are encountered so frequently in reading that it is helpful to learn them very quickly, even before the rules for sounding them out have been mastered. Many of these words will already be familiar to your students.

A measure of the number of words the student can read at sight is made by asking her to read from a list of commonly used English words. Present a set of cards to the student with these words on them. Ask her to make two piles: *knowns* and *unknowns*. Have her read to you the pile of words s/he knows. Count those s/he reads correctly. *Her sight vocabulary is _ _ _ _ words.*

> *Note: Many of these common sight words present a particular challenge to children with reading problems. Some are easily reversible (as **on** and **no**); others differ only in subtle ways, such as having one letter in place of another (**came** - **come**). Those marked with an * are the most frequently confused. In order to learn to recognize them easily, remedial students require a great deal of practice with each of these words.*

A list[X] of commonly used English words is shown below.

the	in	one	she	about	can
of	*that	you	*there	into	only
and	is	I	would	*than	there
*was	on	this	*their	him	new
s/he	be	had	we	been	some
*for	at	not	if	has	could
it	by	are	out	*when	time
with	or	but	so	who	these
as	have	*from	said	will	read
his	an	were	*what	more	may
to	*they	her	up	*no	*then

X The foregoing list of sight words is from *Pope-Dinola Word Bank*, Pope, L. and Dinola, A., Newton, N.J., New Directions Press, 1977

a	which	all	its	*them	do
first	should	*never	though	city	love
any	because	day	pretty	give	full
my	each	same	*went	let	am
*now	just	another	say	big	girl
like	those	know	call	eat	walk
our	people	thank	school	*saw	draw
over	*how	us	*every	best	*run
man	too	great	don't	*ever	black
me	little	old	does	light	play
*even	please	year	get	thing	soon
*most	good	off	left	*want	try
made	very	*come	buy	done	woman
after	make	go	*always	open	exit
did	still	*came	*alway	kind	today
many	own	right	funny	help	two
before	see	take	put	show	danger
*must	stop	bring	think	write	poison
through	work	house	enough	gave	keep
back	long	use	far	today	seem
*where	get	again	better	white	send
much	here	goes	why	tell	
your	between	around	find	together	
way	start	home	going	keep	
well	both	small	look	boy	
down	under	found	ask	peace	

III. Can s/he hear the initial consonants? (Auditory Recognition of Initial Consonants)

Say, "I shall say a word to you. Write the sound that you hear at the beginning of the word." Samples: (b) **boy**; (s) **seem**.

If the student fails to write correctly ten of the sounds, ask her to repeat the sounds to you. Thus you will know whether s/he hears the sound correctly, even though s/he is not yet able to write the letters associated with the sounds.

1. (d)	daily		8. (j)	jam
2. (g)	gown		9. (r)	rabbit
3. (s)	sober		10. (b)	barber
4. (m)	marry		11. (p)	pile
5. (f)	fish		12. (1)	lazy
6. (h)	happy		13. (n)	naughty
7. (c)	cat			

IV. Can s/he hear the final consonants? (Auditory Recognition of Final Consonants)

Say, "I shall say a word to you. Write the sound that you hear at the end of the word." samples: **rap** (p); **leg** (g).

Follow the instructions given for section III.

1. bird (d)	5. half (f)	9. sedan (n)
2. dialogue (g)	6. topaz (z)	10. fight (t)
3. miss (s)	7. lock (c,k)	11. robe (b)
4. stream (m)	8. boil (l)	12. soup (p)

V. Can s/he blend separate sounds to form a word?

I will say two sounds. You tell me what word they could make. **a t.** At is correct. Let's try one more. **Th ing**. Thing is correct. Now try these."

l ip	ro b	s ell	f a n
t op	c u ff	bi n	m e t

VI. Can s/he recognize the consonants and associate the correct sounds with them? (Visual Recognition of Consonants)

Print the consonants on individual cards. Present each card, saying, "These letters have sounds. Can you sound them?"

When you present the letters (c) and (g), remember that each has two sounds. If the student gives one of the proper sounds, tell her that is correct, and ask if s/he also knows another sound for that letter.

If the student finds it difficult to sound the letters, say "Can you think of a word that starts with this sound?"

List the responses in the appropriate columns below.

VII. Can s/he read the short vowel sounds in words?

Print each pair of words on a card.

Correct	Hesitant	Incorrect

Present the cards to the student to read.

fed	lag	rot	lit
fad	lug	rut	lot
fin	rip	lip	gam
fen	rap	lop	gum

VIII. Can s/he read the short and long vowels? (Reading Knowledge of Vowels)

"Read these words as well as you can." Present each word on a separate card.

| 1. mat | 3. let | 5. bin | 7. rob | 9. fun |
| 2. mate | 4. mete | 6. fine | 8. robe | 10. fume |

IX. Does s/he reverse?

Present the following words on cards and say "Read these words."

1. pal	4. tar	7. tops	10. even	13. won	16. read
2. no	5. pot	8. meat	11. saw	14. rats	17. lap
3. raw	6. keep	9. never	12. tan	l5. nap	18. was

X. Can s/he hear the consonant combinations? (Auditory Recognition of Consonant Blends and Digraphs)

Say, "I shall say a word to you. Write the sound that you hear at the beginning of the word. This sound will be a combination of two or more letters." Samples: (**ch**) chicken; (**sp**) speak. Follow the instructions given for Section 3.

1. (**sm**)	smoke	15. (**sk**)	skill
2. (**dr**)	drive	16. (**fl**)	flower
3. (**th**)	thank	17. (**cr, kr**)	rank
4. (**gr**)	grow	18. (**wh**)	wheel
5. (**pl**)	plaster	19. (**scr, skr**)	scream
6. (**gl**)	glue	20. (**sn**)	snore
7. (**sk**)	skate	21. (**fr**)	frank
8. (**ch**)	choose	22. (**spl**)	splendid
9. (**tr**)	trip	23. (**sh**)	shape
10. (**st**)	stand	24. (**spr**)	spring
11. (**pr**)	practice	25. (**br**)	brass
12. (**sl**)	sloop	26. (**sw**)	swing
13. (**str**)	stripe	27. (**bl**)	black
14. (**cl,kl**)	clay	28. (**sp**)	sparrow

XI. Can s/he recognize the consonant combinations? (Visual Recognition of Consonant Blends and Digraphs)

Print the following combinations on separate cards. Present each card to the student, saying, " Can you tell me a word that starts with this sound?"

sh, ch, th, wh, sm, dr, gr, pl, gl, sk, tr, st, pr, sl, str, cl, fl, cr, scr, sn, spl, spr, br, sw, bl, sp

List the responses in the appropriate column below.

Correct	Hesitant	Incorrect

XII. Can s/he read the vowel combinations? (Reading Knowledge of Vowel Combinations including Vowels followed by "r")

Present the following words on cards, saying, "Try to say these words as well as you can, even if you have never seen them before."

1. coal	7. leak	13. lout	19.howl
2. burn	8. avoid	14. maul	20. brew
3. mom	9. nook	15. harm	21. took
4. baw	10. spray	16. mean	22. lie
5. low	11. laid	17. term	
6. free	12. firm	18. joy	

XIII. Can the student separate compound words into their component parts? (Reading Knowledge of Compound Words)

Present the following words on cards, one at a time. "Read these words." After each word has been read, ask, "What were the two words that combined to form this word?"

1. breakfront	5. nevermore	9. senseless
2. cowboy	6. shoplace	10. barefoot
3. anytime	7. grapefruit	
4. grownup	8. grandchild	

XIV. Can s/he read words with prefixes and suffixes attached to the root word? (Reading Knowledge of Prefixes and Suffixes)

Present the following words on cards and request that each one be read. After each one has been read, ask "What do you think that means?" After four words have been read and defined correctly, ask the student how those words were attacked.

1. explain	6. meaner	11. lively
2. unbuckle	7. meanest	12. attendance
3. preview	8. meanness	13. porous
4. disown	9. hopeful	14. seasonal
5. rerun	10. tension	15. rotation

XV. Can the student separate words into syllables to facilitate reading them? (Syllabication)

A. When hearing them:

"I shall say a word to you. Count the syllables in the word—and tell me how many. For example: **syllabicate**. How many syllables did you count?"

mansion	dictionary	friendship
direction	one	amendment
like	twenty	
many	generous	

B. When seeing them:

"Read these words as well as you can, even if you have never seen them before." Present each word on a separate card.

wonderful	knowledge	adrenaline
grandiose	gentlemen	vocabulary
Manchester	introduction	
delight	fantastic	

Teaching Reading

PHILOSOPHIES, METHODS AND TECHNIQUES

Reading, writing, listening and speaking—the language arts—are unique skills that differentiate the human being from all other natural species. They permit human beings to interact socially, to communicate with the past and the future, and to express and enhance thinking and productive development in many areas, including the arts, the sciences and the humanities.

Listening and speaking develop naturally during the child's early years. Reading and writing usually must be taught, although some few children learn these spontaneously.

They are most effectively taught when integrated with speaking and listening, and when the instruction has personal meaning for the student. The Whole Language philosophy of teaching expresses these sentiments and is dedicated to pleasure in learning, in providing a variety of materials with and from which the student can learn, with many opportunities for success. It encourages reading to the student, reading by the student, much writing, and much conversation and discussion. It encourages the use of varied modalities in the learning situation so that, in effect, the student learns from a multi-sensory approach.

Most of the students with whom you will be working have failed, and therefore have had little pleasure in learning; instruction has not been personalized and geared to their interests; and, in many cases, their language experience has been limited. Many have had little contact with good literature—or with lots of conversation.

METHOLOGIES

There are many methods of teaching reading; frequently you will read assertions by one group that they know how to teach reading better than does another group, or that a new method of teaching has been invented. Actually many methods can work with a large majority of students. For the most part, however, you, will be trying to teach students with whom some particular method has not worked. Several of the leading methods will be described to you briefly, chiefly to acquaint you with them. Before describing the methods, however, we present the important distinction between developmental reading instruction and remedial reading instruction.

Developmental reading instruction is the term applied to the teaching of reading to students who have not been taught those skills before. Ordinarily, you will be giving developmental reading instruction only to a very small group of adults—those who are trying to learn to read for the first time and who have never been exposed to any kind of reading instruction.

Remedial reading instruction, in contrast, is meant for those students who have been exposed to instruction but have failed to learn what was expected of them. Generally, such students have learned something, and have learned it unevenly. Nearly all the people you will teach are in this category. With this group it is especially important to determine just what each one has learned and what s/he has not learned—in other words, to use diagnostic teaching.

The skills of reading may be taught in several ways, as needed by each student. Above all, the learning must be associated with as much pleasure as possible. The pleasure will result for the student's feelings of success and progress, from the enjoyment of the stories and ideas that come from the printed word (in literature or the press), and from the respect and supportive relationships among teachers and students.

The Whole Language Approach

The Whole Language Approach has captured the imagination and interest of many teachers who wish to associate pleasure with learning, and who wish to minimize the traditional tedium of the classroom. They bring many fine books into the classroom, encourage learners to explore them, and they make every effort to make learning "fun", as it should be. Although at the onset Whole Language enthusiasts avoided giving direct instructions in phonics, more and more of them now realize that phonics instruction is a necessary part of learning to read for many students; they incorporate the teaching of phonics into their program, while focusing on good literature and fun in learning.

Teaching Sight-Words, or the Look-Say Techniques

This method emphasizes the learning of whole words by recognition of the appearance of the total word. Each word must be memorized independently. More than 200 words in the English language are used so frequently that it is important for the beginning reader to recognize them automatically; knowing these common sight words, or basic sight words, makes it possible to read and understand meaningful material early. See pages 91-92 for a list of these words. Languages using ideographic writing, such as Chinese, must be learned exclusively by this method. Little children who watch TV learn many of the words in the commercials by this method. In school, when this approach is used, the intent is to give the child early satisfaction in getting meaning from the material s/he reads. Picture and context clues are helpful in recognizing words taught by the sight-word method. When enough words have been learned, it becomes important for the learner to acquire phonic skills so that s/he may know the rules by which s/he may expand her reading vocabulary. It is obviously impossible, and unnecessary, to commit the whole language to memory by sight.

Decoding Skills

The decoding approach emphasizes the sounding out of words. Rules are taught for sounding individual letters and combinations of letters. By applying the rules, the student is able to sound out the words. For example, if, when confronted with the letters l-a-t-e, the student has already learned that the final "e" is silent, giving the "a" the long "a" sound, s/he can sound out this word correctly. Since English is not a completely phonetic language, there are many exceptions to the rules. Nevertheless, there is enough consistency when the rules are followed for a knowledge of phonics to be essential. The Phonics and the Linguistic Methods are both examples of the decoding approach to beginning reading instruction: both teach the learner to associate sounds with letter symbols in order to "crack the code."

Teaching the learner to decode is part of every good beginning reading program. To minimize failure, and to remediate those who have failed, it is wise to teach the skills of decoding, or sounding out, in simple orderly steps, as well as when the learner seems confused or puzzled, or needs assistance.

Experience, or Write-Your-Own Book, Technique

This approach is invaluable with adults; it is also used by many teachers to encourage early reading experiences. It is especially valuable in remedial instruction for developing material that is meaningful and interesting to the individual student. The student dictates to the teacher a story or a series of thoughts that has great meaning or interest for her; the teacher writes down the story. If the student is able to write it, or to type it, s/he does so. The story becomes the student's reader; s/he learns the words, s/he reads the story, and s/he expands on it in successive lessons. This is an invaluable method for capturing the interest of someone who has been difficult to reach; the crucial aspect of this method is that of getting to know just which subject is most meaningful to the student. With a child, it may be policemen, or soldiers; with a teenager or an adult, it may be marriage, or the prevalence of drugs, or a special vocational interest, or her own feelings about herself.

The Multisensory Approach

To capture and maintain the student's interest, and at the same time to involve each of the senses in the learning experience, it is important to be sure that the learner sees, hears, touches, smells, tastes, writes, and is involved in doing while learning. For example, the student may hear a recipe for baking chocolate brownies, write the recipe, read it, mix and bake the brownies, inhale their fragrance, and taste them. The student will learn from that lesson, and enjoy it as well.

The Holistic and the Individualized Approach

Recognizing that individuals differ in their skills, their aptitudes, and their interests, many educators in the field of remedial reading attempt to suit the instruction to the individual; they use the method they deem most suitable for each learner, and frequently a combination of all the methods. Some people have superior visual memories, and learn best by seeing. Some have good auditory memories and learn best by hearing and remembering what they hear. Some learn best by using their muscles; they learn best by forming letters with their hands. With some, touch is very helpful; tracing letters with the finger on materials of different textures (sand, velvet, ice) is effective. Some need a combination of these experiences.

To be most effective, the reading teacher should use multisensory appeals; phonics for learning by sounds, sight words for learning by vision, written practice for learning by action, and cut-out letters for the additional use of the sense of touch.

This approach relies on the presence in the classroom of an extensive library of good literature from which the student selects books to read at every opportunity.

Using a combination of approaches insures reaching each student in the learning style best suited for her. It also produces enough variety in the instruction to avoid monotony and to arouse and maintain the student's interest.

Which Method Should You Use?

A. If your supervisor or your agency uses one method or one set of books and directs you to use that one, that is what you should do.

B. If your supervisor does not recommend a particular method, or if there is no supervisor available, study the materials provided for you in the program. These materials will often determine the method you use.

C. If no specific method is prescribed, use the holistic individualized approach following the guidelines set forth here, and making use of references and materials described here. Use your ingenuity, selecting materials on the basis of the interest, attitudes, and ability of the student. Following the student's interests and leads will enrich your instruction. Generally, the emphasis here will be on informal materials that are inexpensive and easily obtained, or on materials created by the teacher.

GENERAL GUIDELINES

After you have some notion of what your student knows and what s/he must learn, set simple goals for her, so that s/he may quickly achieve some success, no matter how small. You should also have some idea of your student's interests. Try to avoid reteaching what s/he already knows; use what s/he knows to help her learn something new. Remember that every lesson must have variety and must be directly related to the interests and needs of the student. Remember that s/he must feel success, and you also must experience success. Remind her of the new things s/he has learned, but do not exaggerate.

For All Students, At All Levels and All Ages

Thinking and Comprehension Skills

The reader, in order to understand what s/he reads, must think about it in order to absorb it. Thinking involves many skills:

- remembering
- relating what one reads, hears or sees to the information and experience one has already absorbed
- noting the order of events (the sequence) in the selection
- carefully analyzing the information, selecting the important or main idea, finding the details, and judging their relative importance
- perceiving similarities and differences between this information and other
- grouping things that are similar in some way, and categorizing them
- inferring a reasonable conclusion from the information
- predicting or anticipating what might happen next
- questioning information and arguments if there is insufficient supporting evidence

- organizing information; putting it in logical order
- interpreting information and events, and seeking a reasonable explanation
- solving problems,
- differentiating between fact and opinion
- differentiating between fantasy and reality
- seeing the relationship between cause and effect
- comparing and contrasting
- figuring out the author's purpose.

Comprehension involves the use of these skills. As the student matures (becomes older and wiser), these skills are used more competently—throughout life. To put it another way, as these skills are used more competently, the student becomes older and wiser.

Because comprehension is an essential part of the reading process, it is important to encourage careful thinking in all conversation and discussion with your students relating to current events, to television and media events, to reading matter or any subject at hand.

Newspapers are a rich source of reading material for your students, and they lend themselves to careful and thoughtful analysis. The sports section, short news items, classified advertisements are particularly interesting to them.

The *who, when, what, where, why* questions are helpful. In addition, ask questions such as:

- What happened first? Next? Next?
- Read part of a book, a story, or watch a VCR. Ask, "What do you think will happen next? How do you think things will work out?" Then compare the student's prediction with the stated outcome.
- Did you like the main character in the story? Why or why not? Were you surprised by anything? Why? Would you have changed the ending? How?
- How are these two (stories, characters, problems, costumes) similar? How are they different?
- Why did this (event) happen? What caused it?
- Why do you think the author wrote this? Do you have any idea from this what kind of person the author is?
- Can you separate the author's opinion from the facts in this piece?

Understanding Language Whose Meaning is Not Literal: Abstract Concepts, Idioms, Metaphors, Colloquial Expressions, Slang

Many of your students will have difficulty in understanding the meanings of words and expressions that are strange to them. For example:

The words **table** and **chair** are understandable, because they can be seen and touched; but your students may have difficulty with words that are abstract, such as **loyalty** and **integrity**. Such words must be defined for them, with many examples of their use.

Expressions such as **my eyes popped** or **when I heard this, my head started to spin** may be confusing to many students, especially young children and those for whom English is a second language. Our spoken and written language are replete with such words and expressions. It is important to be certain that the student understands each of these as they are read or heard; they must be defined, with many examples of their use.

See page 71 for a partial list of non-literal language.

Third Grade Level or Lower

If your student reads at third grade level or lower

- s/he may not yet have acquired the habit of looking at the printed line from left to right
- s/he may not yet recognize enough words at sight
- s/he lacks skill in breaking down long words into smaller familiar units
- her vocabulary may need enlargement
- s/he may be fearful of and disinterested in learning to read

Your goals, then, are to

- build and maintain her interest in acquiring reading skills by associating pleasure and success with the printed word
- teach her to read automatically from left to right
- teach her a basic vocabulary that s/he may recognize at sight
- each her how to sound out unfamiliar words
- teach her to analyze the structure of words as an aid in reading
- help increase her vocabulary
- help increase her comprehension of reading matter

This section contains specific instruction on how to achieve these goals. Read the whole section; then select and use those elements which best meet the needs of your student.

The first step in teaching a student who has not yet mastered the elements of reading is to give her some vocabulary that s/he recognizes at sight. Your student will already know some words that s/he has learned at school or recognizes from TV advertising and daily living. You will help her increase the number of such words. These words will make it possible for her to read meaningful material while s/he is acquiring her sounding-out skills.

At the very same time s/he must be given a systematic method of approaching unfamiliar words. S/he should be taught the sounds of the consistent consonants, the short vowels, the remaining consonants, the long vowels, and then the remaining special sounds. S/he must then learn to break down long words into their component parts as an aid to reading them more easily.

As soon as s/he has learned to sound out the vowels, the student must be given the opportunity to read aloud to the teacher. This will give her the satisfaction of displaying her achievement to himself and the teacher. When the purpose of the lesson is to have the student sound out a word for which s/he has learned the rules, it is important not to read the word for her, but rather to help her figure it out. It is equally important to be tolerant of the student's dialect or foreign accent when s/he is sounding out. Be careful to criticize or correct only when it is obvious that the student has misinterpreted the meaning of the word. Do not correct accent or dialect if the student is reading the word as s/he would ordinarily say it in her own home.

Non-phonetic words (words that do not follow the rules you have taught the student) should be treated as sight words; pronounce them for the student; do not let her try to figure them out. Tell her they are exceptions to the rule.

From the very beginning, it is desirable to include a great deal of writing activity in the teaching. As the student expresses herself in writing, her reading skills are reinforced. Do not criticize spelling errors; your goal at this time is to encourage written expression. If the spelling is criticized, the student may resist writing.

If your student does not always know which is right and which is left, or if s/he does not always read from left to right, spend a few minutes at every session working on this problem, using the activities suggested on page 141.

STEP 1. RECOGNIZING WORDS AT SIGHT

Sight words may be taught by means of the experience approach as well as through the use of word lists. To help the student build a stock of words that s/he recognizes at sight, the vocabulary must be coordinated around her interests. It cannot be emphasized too often that in order for the instruction to be effective, the interest of the student must be captured and maintained continuously. If the student is applying for a job as a clerk, concentrate on words in job applications and on words used in office positions. If the family is planning a wedding, or expecting a baby, the words may be related to those subjects.

Do the same if s/he wants to be a fireman, or an actor, or a truck driver, or if s/he loves food.

The experience approach is helpful with the remedial reader in instruction at every level. Its main technique is the Write-Your-Own-Book, which is essentially a book created by the student for her own reading instruction. The teacher assists in writing down the material.

When no appropriate printed material is available for children and adults, such homemade texts provide a successful substitute. Because the Write-Your-Own-Book is based on the interests and experiences of the individual student, it is particularly meaningful, and thus provides the best motivation that is available to the teacher.

How to Prepare a Write-Your-Own Book

1. First, encourage the student to talk about an interesting or dramatic experience. You may then suggest that the student dictate the story of what happened. The story may be about an interview for a job, or a ball game, or it may be a discussion of automobiles. It may even be about an incident with the landlord or police.

2. Use a felt-tipped or a ball-point pen for the manuscript printing. Typography should be clear, bold and black. Each page should look attractive and neat. If possible, make a carbon copy of the story at the same time, or, if it is more convenient, make a photocopy (Xerox). Reserve the copy for later use.

3. Use the student's natural and colloquial expressions. Do not edit or rewrite excessively. Many students tend to dictate run-on sentences or endless numbers of "and"-connected sentences. Here your guidance is valuable: keep the sentences short. Try to vary the sentence structure. Substitute periods for the "ands" without disturbing the flow of dictation. Provide for repetition of words.

> NOTE: *When the student dictates a contraction (can't, don't), write the word as s/he dictates it. After s/he has reread the story, it will be helpful to point out to her that this is the short form of two words that ordinarily look a little bit different: When written out, "can't" is "cannot," "don't" is "do not."*

4. Clip the story into a folder; the folder becomes the cover for the book. Have the student print a title and her name on the cover. Encourage her to illustrate the cover and the stories, if s/he is a school child, or if you feel s/he has an interest in illustration. When practicable, photographs of the student can be used to heighten the impact of the book.

5. Have the student read the story back to you. In the course of reading the story s/he has just dictated, s/he will be hesitant about some of the unfamiliar words. Tell her those words, and then print each such word on a card. Let the student practice reading the unfamiliar words from the card as well as the book.

6. Depending on the kind of practice that the student needs, cut the carbon copy of her story into words, or phrases, or sentences. Let her read the "cut-ups"; let her rearrange them in new sequences, and read them back in the new order.

7. At the next lesson, review the words with her. Have her reread the story. Discuss it with her. Then, encourage her to dictate a new chapter, for which you follow the procedure just outlined.

Your student's Write-Your-Own-Book may be varied in ways that will make her lessons more interesting. It can be:

- a scrapbook, iillustrated with pictures that s/he draws or cuts out of magazines;
- a book or play that s/he and you write as part of your dramatic play together;
- a newsletter or newspaper for the tutoring center.
- a "how-to" book about something s/he likes to do, such as How to Build a Wooden Scooter." Or "How to Build a Soapbox Wagon," or a cookbook. When making this book, it is perfectly reasonable to perform the activity at the same time, if the tutoring facilities allow for such work as baking or building. Research for the book may involve looking at library manuals, following their instructions, making shopping lists for the necessary materials and equipment, and actually shopping.

Dramatic results are possible with this technique, particularly when a teacher uncovers a subject of great interest to the student. At such times, the student may even learn to read long and difficult words (**elephant, brontosaurus**) before s/he learns the short, commonly used words, such as **this, then, these.**

The experience method is usually coordinated with, or supplementary to, other methods described in Steps 2 and 3.

Word Lists

In addition to the words derived from the Write-Your-Own Book, it is essential to teach as sight words the common words that make up at least 50% of all reading matter. These words are listed in pages 91-92. At each session, a few minutes should be spent learning those words that are still unfamiliar to the student. To provide variety in practicing on these and any other words or sounds the student is learning, several helpful devices are described in pages 148 ff.

Any device or game that will provide interest and variety in practice should be used. Always try to appeal to as many of the senses as possible at every point: pronounce the word; have the student write it, or trace it, or feel its shape after it is cut out of materials of different textures, such as sandpaper or velvet; have the student say it or act it out.

Encourage the beginner to look for words and letters everywhere: to hunt around on the back of tin cans and cereal cartons to find letters and words that s/he recognizes and knows; to look at street signs and posters for numbers that s/he knows, for the letters in her name, and for words that s/he can recognize or sound out as s/he learns phonic skills; and to look at television commercials, magazines, newspapers, and even skywriting, with the same interest and eagerness. Every new recognition should bring with it a feeling of victory.

Abbreviations

Abbreviations are encountered frequently and may be difficult for the student to decipher. They should be taught to her as sight words. Here are some of the more common abbreviations.

P.S.	Public School	p.	page
I.S.	Intermediate School	pp.	pages

J.H.S.	Junior High School	mph	miles per hour
&	and	etc.	et cetera, and so on
Ave.	avenue	c/o	care of
St.	street	A.M.	morning
Blvd.	boulevard	P.M.	afternoon
Mr.	mister	P.S.	postscript
Mrs.	title of a married woman	S.O.S.	cry for help
Ms	miss or mistress		
M.D.	doctor of medicine		
Dr.	doctor	lb.	pound
D.D.S.	doctor of dental surgery	vs.	versus
oz.	ounce	C.O.D.	cash on delivery

In addition, teach the months of the year and the states of the union.

STEP 2. SOUNDING OUT UNFAMILIAR WORDS

Remember that your student already knows some of the letter sounds. Keep a list of those s/he knows, but do not reteach them. In Part 4 you will find Sound-Out Sheets that contain words lists to assist you.

The sounds may be taught in the following order: (1) the consonants whose sounds do not usually vary; (2) the short vowels; (3) the remaining single consonants; (4) the long vowels; (5) the remaining special sounds. For each sound that you teach, the student should learn a key word (see pages 156-163).

The Consonants Whose Sounds Do Not Usually Vary

b, d, f, h, j, k, l, m, n, p, r, s, t, v, w, z

How to Teach a New Sound

a. To teach a new sound, be sure that your student can hear the sound you are teaching, and can distinguish it from other sounds. Before you teach the consonant **b**, have your student isten to the sound of b words: **bill, but, boy**. Then have her select the words that do not begin with the same sound from among those: **ball, bat, bounce, cat, bay**. Have her tell you words that start with the sound of **b**.

b. Now s/he is ready to associate the sound with its letter and with its key words (in this case, **ball**). Write a list of words beginning with **b**. Pronounce each word as you write it. Have her pronounce it, too. Have the student point out in what way the words sound the same and look the same: they all start with the same sound, and the letter that represents that sound at the beginning of each word is **b**. Once more, have her tell you other words that begin with this sound, and list them. Have her write the letter, together with the key word and its illustration, in her notebook.

Avoid giving the sound of any consonant in isolation. If the student learns the sound of the letter **b** as **buh**, it will be difficult for her to blend sounds. It is best to demonstrate the sound of **b** by saying the key word for that sound, **ball**.

c. Involve all of the student's senses in associating the letter with its sound. Have her write it in the air, on the board, on paper, in sand, with clay, or shape it with pipe cleaners, while at the same time saying words that begin with that sound.

d. Now the student is ready to sound out words using the new sound. It is important to use the sound in words as quickly as possible. Present the new letter in words of one syllable, associating it with sounds that s/he already know, so that s/he may blend them together to form a word that s/he can recognize: **bat**.

e. As soon as s/he has learned to read her new sound in words, the student is ready to practice reading that sound in sentences. Prepare sentences that use that sound frequently: **Bob** is at the **bat but Bill begs Ben** to **be** a **bit better**.

It is important to keep in mind that some students have difficulty learning new sounds; they need a great deal of practice and repetition; and their tutors need a great deal of patience.

The Short Vowels

After several of the consistent consonants with their key words have been taught, the student is ready to learn the short vowels.

Start by teaching the short **a** sound, together with its key word, **apple.** The student is then shown how this sound, placed between the sounds of two of the consonants s/he knows, makes a word: s/he can now sound out the words **f-a-t** and **b-a-n**. It is important to help her blend the sounds smoothly, to hold one sound until next one is begun, and for her to feel satisfaction at the recognition of a word that s/he can now read for the first time.

S/he should practice blending, using her known consonants and the short **a**, as in:

tap   sad   man   dab   pan

Additional word lists are on pages 152 ff..

After the **a**, introduce the short **i** sound. It can be taught in the same way, using

pin   sip   mid   fit   hip

Review the **a** and the **i** sounds by presenting a list of mixed words;

man him lit fan pin nip ran sad bit had

Teach the sound of short **u**.

jut   bun   rub   mud   pup

Review the three short vowels together.

jut lip rat ran sat bun mud fun sip

Following this, teach the short **e.** Many children find it difficult to differentiate between the short **i** and the short **e** sounds.

net　　　fed　　　hen　　　set　　　leg

Review the four short vowels.

man　pen　lit　pin　ran　net　jut　him　sad

Teach the sound of the short **o**

hop　　　dot　　　bob　　　not　　　rot

Review all the short vowel sounds

kit　　　not　　　set　　　ran　　　sun　　　pat
rob　　　hen　　　tin　　　bun　　　man　　　sot　　　mill

The Remaining Single Consonant Sounds

The student is now ready to learn the remaining consonant sounds, with the key words, and to use them in blending with the vowels.

c as in cat　　　　**c** as in cent
g as in gallon　　　**g** as in gin

The sound of **y** as in yet and of **q** and **x** may be taught during the course of instruction when the need arises.

The Long Vowel Sounds

Because the sounds of the long vowels are the same as the names of the vowels, the student will have little difficulty learning the sounds. S/he must, however, learn the following instances of when to use the long vowel sounds.

1. The **e** at the end of a word is always silent, giving the preceding vowel the long sound.

fine　　　rave　　　pure　　　lone　　　sake　　　mete

2. In words where one vowel follows another, the first vowel sound is pronounced by name and the second vowel is silent, as in the following double vowel words.

deem   meat   rain   oak   need

Other Special Sounds

Consonant Combinations. Teach common consonant combinations:

sl, pr, cr, fr, br, tw, pl, cl, bl, fl, gl, sc, sk, sm, sn, sw, gr, tr, dr, sp, st, spl, spr, str, nk, ng, nt, nd

Lists of words using these combinations are on pages   .

Additional Consonant Sounds. The student must learn the additional consonant sounds formed by **sh, ch, th,** and **wh**. Even though each of these is a pair of letters, the pair represents one sound, and is treated as one sound. The consonant sounds of **ph** and **ng** and **gh**, that do not occur as frequently, may be taught as the need arises during reading instruction.

sh	shop	fish	shell	shape	cash
ch	chin	chip	chop	chat	hill
th	thing	thick	thin	think	thank
wh	whiff	which	when	wheel	while

Review the special consonant sounds.

| shape | play | chip | clock | thing | skin | spot |
| blow | flame | whip | glass | grow | pray | stiff |

Additional Vowel Sounds. As the need arises, special vowel sounds should be taught to the student. At that time, systematic practice in these sounds should be given. (See word lists in Part 4).

oo	as in soon	**ow**	as in slow
oo	as in book	**au**	as in maul
oi	as in oil	**ay**	as in day
ow	as in owl	**y**	as in my
ar	as in bar	**or**	as in for
ir	as in fir	**er**	as in her
ur	as in burn		

STEP 3. ANALYZING THE PARTS OF WORDS

By learning how to break down words into their parts, your student also learns to build new words into her reading and speaking vocabulary. This should be taught directly after sound blending has been mastered. Fluent readers learn to recognize frequently occurring prefixes, suffixes and roots, and to combine the parts of compound words.

Compound Words

Sometimes a student who can read single words is confused when these words are put together to form compound words; for her the compound word is a new word pattern. S/he must be helped to see compound works as two words put together. Have her practice reading the parts, and then the whole words:

news	paper	newspaper
can	not	cannot
farm	house	farmhouse
cow	boy	cowboy
grand	child	grandchild

See p. 182 for a helpful list of compound words.

Base, or Root Words, and Common Word Endings

To help identify base, or root, words, list a number of sets of words that have common roots. Have the student find the base word of each of the following;

asked	asking	asks	
rained	raining	rainy	
helps	helping	helpful	helper
farmed	farming	farmer	farms
running	runs	runner	
sleeping	sleeps	sleepy	

Make up exercises in which the student fills in the appropriate base word and ending. Use the base word sing:

John is a good ____.

Jane ___ well.

Tom is ___ a hymn.

Prefixes

Prefixes must be recognized as units, separated visually from the rest of the word. It is important for the reader to learn the meaning of the prefix, so that s/he may know how it alters the meaning of the base word.

When the prefix or suffix is attached to a word whose meaning one already understands, it will be easy to understand the total word (the base word, with a prefix or suffix attached to it.)

It is very important to have a dictionary nearby. Encourage her to look up in the dictionary every word that is not clear. Read the newspapers; read easy books; read books that are more difficult. Make a list of the words that the student does not understand in the paragraph that s/he has read. Have her read the paragraph once more, and s/he will understand it more fully.

Note how the prefixes placed before the words in each of the following columns change the meaning of the words.

re	dis	un
fill	like	even
tell	appear	true
read	approve	fit
write	courage	lucky
print	agree	happy

Following is a list of some of the common prefixes, together with their usual meanings, and with examples of words in which they are used.

in means *not*, as in

informal
inhuman
insincere
incorrect
invisible

in also means *into, inside*, as in

income
indoor
inland

dis means *not* or *the opposite of*, as in

dislike
distrust
disarm
disagree
disorder
disappear

en means *in, into, make*, as in

enable
enforce
enclose
enlighten
enjoy
enlarge

ex means *out, out of*, as in

expel
exit
exhaust

pre means *before*, as in

prehistoric
preview
prepaid

re means *again.* as in

- repeal
- repeat
- recall
- recharge
- renew
- review
- reclaim
- replant

un means *not,* as in

- unwise
- unsound
- untidy
- uneven
- unjust
- uneasy

con means *with, together,* as in

- conduct
- condense
- confederation
- conform
- confront

dis means *out, out of,* as in

- disown
- dispossess
- disease
- dislocate
- disrobe

Suffixes

Suffixes should be taught in the same manner as prefixes. The common suffixes are **-ly, -er, -est, -tion, -ness, -ful, -less, -ous, -ious, -ent,** and **-ment**. Note how the suffixes placed after the words in each of the following columns create new words.

ful	ly	ment	less	est	er	ous
wonder	quick	enjoy	sleep	tall	tall	joy
care	sweet	settle	pain	slow	slow	poison
help	kind	improve	thought	fast	fast	marvel
thought	slow	agree	help	strong	strong	glory

As you expect, **ful** means *full*, as in

skillful
powerful
restful
frightful

tion describes a condition, or the process of, or the product of doing what is described by the base word:

attraction
collection
digestion
connection
exception

ness means the state of being *bright, plain* or whatever word it is attached to:

brightness
plainness
hickness
readiness
likeness

ment describes the product of doing the activity that is described by the base word:

achievement
investment

Dividing Words into Syllables

Your pupil need not know all the rules of syllabication, but s/he should have some understanding of how to reduce a long word to its simple elements and so read it more easily.

S/he must first know that every syllable must have one vowel sound, and that each vowel sound identifies one syllable. S/he may therefore listen to a word, count the number of vowel sounds, and thus know the number of syllables. Since only vowel sounds count, silent vowels are to be ignored. Double vowels (**oo**, **ee**) have one vowel sound, as do special vowel combinations, such as **ou**, **ow**, **oi**, **oy**, **ay**, **au**, **aw**.

The teacher may recite unfamiliar long words to the student, and have the student count the syllables. After the student has earned to count the syllables in a word, s/he is ready to divide words into syllables. S/he is now ready for these simple rules:

1. When two consonants are between two vowels, the syllables are divided between the consonants.

af ter   les son   bas ket   num ber

2. When a word has a vowel-consonant-vowel sequence, the consonant is usually part of the first syllable if the first vowel is short (see column A.) It is part of the second syllable if the first vowel is long (see column B).

A	B
pris on	e vil
tax i	mu sic
	si lent

3. When **le** is at the end of a word of more than one syllable, the last consonant joins the **le** to make the last syllable:

ta ble	trem ble	stum ble
bu gle	rat tle	puz zle

STEP 4. ENCOURAGING THE STUDENT TO READ A STORY

Both oral and silent reading are important. When the student reads orally, you are able to hear her hesitations and her errors, and to help her when s/he is stuck. However, s/he may be embarrassed to hear herself stumble, and may be unable to concentrate on the meaning while s/he reads aloud slowly.

Silent reading is valuable as well. The student reads more quickly, is less embarrassed, and, even when s/he meets an unknown word that s/he cannot sound out, often understands its meaning from the context.

When your student is able to read printed text, encourage her to do so, orally and silently, as you judge best for that student at that time.

Some readers mumble to themselves as they read silently, or form the words with their lips. Do not discourage them from doing so. When they no longer need this crutch, they will drop it.

To minimize anxiety in the student who lacks confidence in reading, it may be helpful to

a. Allow her to read the passage or story silently before reading it aloud.

b. Take turns; you read one line or sentence, and s/he reads the next one.

c. Have the student read the selection into a tape recorder and then hear herself.

d. When appropriate, dramatize the selection. Each of you plays the parts portrayed in the selection.

e. Discuss the selection with the student before s/he reads it.
Discuss the place, the theme, what to look for or what to expect.

f. Interrupt the reading as little as possible. Interruptions will interfere with concentration—s/he will then not remember what s/he is reading. If s/he has great difficulty figuring out a word, tell it to her (do not let her struggle with it at this time, even though you are positive that s/he can figure it out.) Overlook insignificant errors that do not change the meaning of the selection: house for home, for example.

g. After reading the selection, discuss it with her. What was it about? Does it make sense? What happened first? And then what? And then? Why? If the student has difficulty answering any one of your questions, offer help within a few seconds. Otherwise, s/he will feel stupid.

YOUR GOAL IS TO GIVE THE STUDENT A FEELING
OF SUCCESS AND PLEASURE. REMEMBER THAT.

STEP 5. DEVELOPING COMPREHENSION SKILLS

The reader must understand what s/he reads in order to enjoy it and use it academically, vocationally, and in everyday life. Teaching comprehension skills is therefore a vital part of reading instruction at every level.

Even in the early stages of instruction, the student understands a great deal more than s/he is able to read. Her speaking vocabulary, concepts, and experience are often ahead of her ability to decipher the written symbol. After s/he has mastered the mechanics of reading, the emphasis in instruction should shift to increasing understanding. From this point on, increasing her reading level means increasing her vocabulary and ability to read and interpret more and more difficult material.

The students you teach, because of their histories of school failure and their resistance to formal learning, are all too ready to give up. The reading matter they use must be meaningful, absorbing, and useful to engage and hold their interest and attention. If it fails to involve them, they will drop instruction as soon as they have mastered the minimal skills necessary for their immediate specific goals, such as reading the subway signs, passing the driver's test, or filling out a job application. This means that the tutor must select materials for each student according to her needs, interests, and level of competence.

No matter what her age, your student has by this time acquired enough experience and vocabulary to understand a great deal about the world. Although s/he is unable to read the words s/he knows, s/he is able to expand her listening and speaking vocabulary.

Activities

A list of comprehension and study skills to be taught to all students is on pages 103-105. Suggestions on how you may teach these skills at and below the fourth grade level follow.

Comprehension, as well as vocabulary, is sharpened through the use of oral discussion. Aim at clarity of thought and observation on the part of the student as you conduct the first three activities.

Useful activities include:

1. Discussions centering on current matters of interest to the student (housing, election issues, medical care, civil rights, play, toys, job-seeking and job-related problems, hobbies, personal interests).

2 Discussions relating to mass media that reach the student (a radio program s/he heard or that the tutor recommended to her, a TV program, a picture magazine article, a movie).

3. Discussions relating to visits, made with or without the tutor, in which the student discovers new things, or sees new aspects of old things, such as museums, factories, zoos and parks.

4. Reading to the student by the teacher using material of interest to her.

5. Making lists of words in interesting categories to increase vocabulary. For example, compile a list of words for preparing meals (**food**, **sugar**, **meat**, **stove**, **oven**, **temperature**), for repairing automobiles (**car**, **engine**, **carburetor**, **mile**, **mileage**), or for the soldier (**greetings**, **induction**, **soldier**, **marine**).

6. Using the student's own slang or colloquial language to help increase her vocabulary. Make a dictionary translating her words into those in more common usage; do not discourage her from continuing to use her colloquial expression, but instead assist in expanding her vocabulary based on these special words. Thus, **cool**, **hep**, and **jive** can be translated. These words the student uses may be unfamiliar to you. S/he will translate them for you. You will find your own vocabulary expanding.

Following are specific comprehension skills that the student should aim at developing, with suggested activities. Particular attention should be given to the techniques that improve clarity of thinking.

A. Selecting the main idea:

Make up a title for a story, discussion, TV, or radio program.

Select the best of several titles.

Tell (or write at the student's level) a summary of the story or discussion.

Select the most important sentence of the paragraph.

B. Organization of ideas:

Tell what happened in chronological order.

Tell what happened in logical order.

Organize simple sentences in the correct order.

Organize simple paragraphs in the correct order.

Find the answers to the questions **who, what, when, where, why** and **how**.

C. Finding details:

Find the answers to specific questions.

Fill in details that have been omitted in a report or discussion of a book, program or trip.

D. Reading directions:

Have the student follow your directions. These should be very simple at first and become more complicated as time goes on.

Directions may involve how to find a book in the room, or another room in the building, on how to travel to a special place, or how to follow a simple construction job, a simple drawing.

Have the student give you directions for any simple project like one of the foregoing. Be sure they are complete and can be followed; if unclear, have her fill in the missing details.

In all cases, these directions should flow from the teacher/student interaction and the interests of the teacher and of the student.

E. Drawing inferences:

Complete a story.

Anticipate what will happen next in a story, or in current events.

Draw conclusions from information given.

Interpret the meaning of a sentence or a paragraph.

Materials

In addition to the commercial reading materials listed in Part IB, the following sources are helpful:

- Daily newspapers
- *News for You*, New Readers Press, Syracuse, New York. This is high interest-level, low reading-level weekly newspaper published in Spanish and English editions for use with adult beginning readers.
- Write-Your-Own Book dictated by student
- News telecasts and radio news broadcasts
- Picture, sports and hobby magazines, such as *Ebony, Popular Mechanics, Sports Illustrated*
- Vocational material simplified by teacher
- Catalogues: mail order, sports, etc.
- Technical manuals
- Cook books

STEP 6. ENCOURAGING WRITING SKILLS

Written work and pride in composition should be developed at this time through the Write-Your-Own Book, as explained earlier on page 108.

Be careful when assigning written reports or compositions to students at this reading level. Such assignments are difficult and should not be allowed to spoil what should be an enjoyable and rewarding experience. Many students lack confidence in their writing skills, and are reluctant to express themselves. Encourage them to write notes, memos and letters. Praise every effort, and tolerate errors and omissions as they begin to write. As they gain confidence, they will be able to tolerate corrections and suggestions.

Fourth to Eighth Grade Levels

If your student reads at fourth to eighth grade levels

- s/he needs help in reading for pleasure
- s/he needs help in reading for understanding
- s/he needs help in learning how to study
- s/he may still have some weakness in sounding out words
- s/he may make some of the common reading errors
- her vocabulary requires expansion

Your goals, then, are to

- help maintain her interest in reading
- help correct her weaknesses in sounding out words
- help break down the patterns that cause her to make common errors
- help increase her vocabulary
- teach comprehension and study skills

Remember that the student's interest level is higher than her reading level. Until s/he is able to read easily the material that is satisfying and useful to her, it is your responsibility to motivate her to remain with the program. It is your job to retain her interest despite the difficulty in locating appropriate materials. If you can assure her (truthfully) that s/he is making progress, s/he may be satisfied with material that is not particularly interesting to her.

Look through any material you select before giving it to your student. You may find the subject matter inappropriate, and in some cases, offensive; if so, discard it. (For example, one of the adult basic readers speaks disparagingly of work done by a porter. It is obviously destructive to present such reading matter to a student who is at present interested in or occupied in such work, or to a young person whose father may be so occupied). Try to avoid graded readers designed for young children. Also avoid reading matter that is frustratingly difficult.

If your student is fourteen years of age or older, select vocationally-oriented material. If you know your student, you will know what to look for.

You will be working on the same skill as those listed for the beginning reader on page 106, but at a higher level. At this level the student should read the material himself, when possible. Your lessons should include practice designed to correct any errors that your student makes (see pages 141 ff.).

1. Vocabulary can be expanded at this level by teaching the use of the dictionary. Look up the meanings of words as they occur in conversation or in the reading matter. The dictionary then becomes a useful and friendly tool. Activities should include alphabetizing, finding several definitions for the same word, and analyzing the meanings of words in which the prefixes are varied, the roots are changed, or the suffixes are changed. In addition, continue to emphasize comprehension in listening, in reading, and in discussing, and begin to teach study skills.

2. Comprehension skills will be developed further by the activities described in the previous section (page 123). At the present level, clarity of thought should also be emphasized, using the following techniques:

- Make outlines of paragraphs, stories, programs, and discussions.
- Fill in simple outlines.
- Find the author's point of view.
- Select the words and phrases that are editorial rather than reportage in news items.
- Differentiate between subjective and objective statements.
- Seek evidence for information, when appropriate.
- Identify emotionally loaded words and phrases.
- Read several accounts of the same event or subject and compare them.

3. Study skills may be developed through teaching the following:

- How to use the title page, table of contents, index
- How to use the dictionary

- How to use the library
- How to take notes on books and on class discussion
- How to make an outline

Materials suggested on page 136 and those listed in the Helpful Publications section (page 212) should be used.

THE WRITING PROCESS

Spelling, writing, and speaking skills develop as reading competence advances. At first, compositions are dictated to the teacher. This is done when the task of writing is difficult for the student. If asked to write, s/he may be unable to express the ideas that s/he is able to dictate. But, as her reading skill improves, so will her ability to write. At that time, s/he should be encouraged to write brief paragraphs that s/he will later develop into longer compositions. Let her write about the things s/he likes: describe a person s/he likes or dislikes, write a story about her wishes or about her best friend; describe a job; tell about a conversation at the neighborhood candy store; write a song; tell what s/he would do if s/he were a landlord, or the principal of a school; write about anything of interest to her or to you.

To encourage self-expression, teaching must use the utmost tact and be protective of the feelings of the student. Some errors should be overlooked, if you wish to encourage expression. Concentrate on vocabulary usage and improved organization of ideas. Overlook spelling errors; they may be relatively unimportant at this time. It is not necessary that you criticize every weakness in every piece of writing. It is far better to say, "We'll work on spelling at some other time," to indicate to the student that, although the spelling is incorrect, the composition has merit. Remember that encouragement and sincere commendation for improvement and for work well done are the most effective incentives for continued progress.

Many students have little confidence in knowing enough about any subject to write about it, and are totally resistant to expressing themselves in writing. They feel inadequate in spelling, in information, and in the use of expressive language. They need encouragement, support and assistance in realizing how much information they already have, and in knowing how to get more information, if necessary; and then they need guidance in how to organize that information so that they can write about it.

a. **Brainstorming** is the first step. Choose a subject: **pet dogs**, for example, or **Holland**, or **medical costs**, or **my favorite teacher**. Talk about it, listing every thought and every bit of information that comes out of the discussion. Make the list as you go along.

b. **Organizing** is the next step. Help the student put the list in logical order. This can be done by writing numbers in front of the items, without rewriting the list: No. 1 for the first point, No. 2 for the next point, etc. Sometimes it is helpful to the student to rewrite the list in logical order, instead of numbering the points. Actually, this list has become an outline for the written work that s/he is about to do.

c. **Writing** is next. The student now writes her thoughts, following the outline. Ignore misspellings. Your goal now is to encourage her to put words and thoughts on paper.

d. **Rewriting or Revising** is then essential. Students resist rereading and revising their written work, which they were reluctant to do in the first place. They need encouragement to look for the following:

• Did the writer say what s/he wanted to say?
• Does it make sense?
• Is it clear?

e. **The finishing touches**. Although spelling, punctuation, and legible handwriting are all very important, it may be necessary for you to overlook these areas with some of your students at this point, particularly young children. Work on these details may be the "last straw" for resistant writers, and discourage them completely. They may see them as criticisms that brand them as failures once more. The sensitive teacher will know which students are prepared for this step.

Ninth Grade Level or Better

Students who read at the ninth-grade level and have returned for remedial instruction are probably aware that, in order to qualify for technical occupations, a high school diploma or its equivalent (the high school equivalency certificate) is necessary. Instruction for this group involves no new skills, but rather the further development of the skills taught earlier, such as increased vocabulary, heightened understanding of material read, greater critical evaluation, better study skills, and greater appreciation and enjoyment of the printed word.

1. VOCABULARY

Vocabulary is increased by helping establish the habit of looking up words in the dictionary and by increased concentration on technical vocabulary. Keep vocabulary lists in a book or card file.

2. COMPREHENSION

After the mechanical aspects of reading have been mastered, comprehension skills are further developed through increased understanding and use of the printed page. Reading instruction now concentrates on helping the student understand and interpret what s/he reads.

Understanding and Interpreting Meaning

Each of the following processes and skills is involved in the comprehension of written matter:

- Understanding literal meaning of words, sentences, selections
- Understanding the meaning of punctuation marks
- Relating the story: telling what happened first, what happened then, and what happened last
- Getting the main thought
- Finding details
- Following instructions
- Seeing relationships and making comparisons; seeing cause and effect
- Predicting outcomes and solutions
- Understanding the meaning of figurative language

• Drawing conclusions

• Making generalizations

Critical Reading

In order to read with discrimination, the student should have guidance and practice the following:

• Distinguishing the significant from the trivial, relevant from irrelevant, fact from opinion
• Evaluating material read from the reader's own experience and from other criteria
• Determining the writer's point of view
• Reading widely on controversial issues
• Maintaining an objective and inquiring point of view
• Looking for use of propaganda devices,: bandwagon, "loading the dice," glad words, bad words, glittering generalities, "plain folks."

3. STUDY SKILLS

Study skills can be advanced through all the activities listed for earlier levels, as well as by encouraging the use of almanacs, atlases, and encyclopedias. Students may be led to use these reference works by having them pursue and report on interesting research projects, such as occupational surveys, the salaries of typists, the prices asked for used cars of different makes, models or years, or the number of bricklayers employed in successive decades.

Many who read well are unfortunately unable to use their reading to learn. They therefore require instruction and practice in the following study skills:

Basic Study Skills

• alphabetizing
• locating Information through the use of the title page and table of contents

- reading maps, diagrams
- using the glossary and index
- using the dictionary
- using the encyclopedia and other reference materials
- understanding graphs and tables
- understanding the bibliography
- using the library catalog

Organizing Information

- listing
- classifying
- inding main ideas
- selecting important details
- skimming to find specific information
- summarizing
- outlining
- note-taking
- rereading to aid in retention

Learning How to Study

- note-taking
- outlining
- reviewing
- anticipating questions and formulating answers

Committing Information to Memory

- practicing, with intervals between each practice or study period.
- continuing to practice until the response is automatic

Test-Taking

- overviewing the test
- judging how to allocate time for each question
- making judgment of whether guessing is penalized on this particular test.

4. HOW TO PREPARE AN OUTLINE FOR A REPORT

I. Introduction

Many students are overwhelmed by an assignment to prepare a report, even though they possess the competence and technical skills to read the required material, to gather the necessary information, and to organize it properly. They need guidance in how to prepare an outline. An outline is an orderly arrangement of ideas and information. It helps to clarify ideas and to facilitate their recall by establishing relationships among them. The outline may be sketchy or detailed, depending on how it is to be used. The development of a sample outline is described on page 130. A more formal outline is described here.

II. Purpose:

A. To organize ideas and information for study and recall.
B. To organize ideas and information for the preparation of a written report or an oral presentation.

III. Procedure:

A. Preparation
1. In preparing an outline of material that the student hears, s/he must take notes and then treat those notes as though they were reading matter.
2. To prepare an outline of material that s/he reads, the student should first skim the selection to get an overview of it, and then read the selection carefully, outlining it as s/he reads it. See below for further instructions.
3. To prepare an outline for a written or oral presentation that

s/he will make, the student should list her thoughts, ideas and facts in a legible fashion. S/he should then reorganize them into an outline.

Sometimes it is helpful if the teacher or the tutor asks leading questions to encourage the student in expressing her thoughts and ideas.

B. Preliminary Thinking About Ideas and Details
1. Identify the central theme.
2. Identify the main ideas.
3. Identify the details that support the main ideas.
   a. Sometimes they illustrate the main idea.
   b. Sometimes they explain the main idea.
   c. Sometimes they give reasons for or causes of the main idea.
   d. Sometimes they give chronological or sequential development of events of the main idea, or relating to the main idea.
   e. Sometimes they give definitions of the main idea.
4. Identify the relationships among the ideas.

C. Writing the Outline
1. Organize the facts and ideas according to
   a. Sequence, or
   b. Importance, or
   c. Any relationship that you have selected
2. Insert supportive details (or facts) in the appropriate section, according to the organization you have selected.
3. Consolidate outline by
   a. Combining ideas that are similar
   b. Discarding minor or inconsequential details
   c. Discarding irrelevant thoughts or data
   d. Avoiding repetition:
4. Form of the Outline
   a. To indicate parallel and subordinate relationships easily, it is helpful to use a combination of letters and numerals in outlining.
      i. Roman Numerals—main thoughts or ideas: I, II
      ii. Letters—major details: A, B, C
      iii. Arabic Numerals—minor details: 1, 2, 3
      iv. Lower Case Letters—subordinate details: a, b, c.

    b. Subheadings may be added to clarify the meanings of headings.

    c. Each item is indented according to its importance. All listings of the same letter or numeral carry parallel or similar weight or value in terms of their relationships within the outline.

5. MATERIALS

At this level, a great deal of reading matter is available. Encourage reading of all types of material. Allow ample time for discussion. Do not discourage the reading of pulp magazines or tabloid newspapers: any reading that is successful and enjoyable helps develop reading power. As a result of your discussions and the reading matter that you can locate at the library, the reading taste of your student will be improved, and s/he will learn to appreciate fine literature

Remember to use:

- Daily newspapers
- Magazines: picture magazines, digests, women's magazines, special interest magazines
- Paperback book clubs: Scholastic Press (very inexpensive editions)
- *G. E. D. High School Equivalency Exam*, Arco Publishing Co., New York.
This book is excellent for the development of comprehension and study skills; it is most useful for those interested in taking the examination to be discussed next. The book also provides opportunity for practice in taking tests, essential for your student at this point.

6. GENERAL EDUCATIONAL DEVELOPMENT (GED) TESTS

The General Educational Development (GED) Tests have enabled millions of adults to earn high school equivalency diplomas. With a diploma, the student can take advantage of education and training above the high school level, and improve her earning potential.

High school equivalency programs were launched in most states after World War II to enable veterans to earn high school diplomas. The programs have been extended to include civilian adults who, having failed to complete their educations, may desire formal accreditation of their training. The high school equivalency diploma is the legal equivalent of a high school diploma for purposes of civil service requirements. It is normally accepted by business concerns and the Armed Forces as the equivalent of the high school diploma. Some colleges will accept the certificate for admission; inquiries should be made directly to the college of choice.

Information on how to file for high school equivalency tests is available from all local high schools and from the state education departments. Although examinations are given frequently, there is a waiting list in some states. It is therefore advisable to file early, and then to embark on a course of study for the examination. Your students reading at or above the ninth-grade level should be encouraged to prepare for this examination. It is a realistic goal for them, and one well worth achieving.

The GED tests are designed to judge whether the student has the skills in literacy and computation equal to the upper two-thirds of those now graduating from high schools in the United States. About 800,000 adults take the GED test each year, and well over 500,000 of them are awarded high school equivalency diplomas.

The English language GED battery consists of five individual tests:

Test 1: Writing Skills

    Section A: Finding errors in sentence structure, usage, capitalization, punctuation, spelling, etc.

    Section B: An essay writing exercise: writing a composition of about 200 words giving an opinion or explaining an issue.

Test 2: Reading Skills: Interpreting Literature and the Arts: a test of ability to read and interpret passages.

Test 3: Social Studies. 64 questions.

Test 4: Science. 66 Questions.

In Social Studies and Science, questions test one's ability to think, rather than simply to memorize the facts. Questions seek to find out whether one can

    a. comprehend new information
    b. apply what has been learned
    c. analyze a new idea by breaking it into parts
    d. evaluate items and make judgments about them

Test 5: Mathematics. Questions test skills including

    a. solving number problems

    b. solving graph problems

    c. deciding whether a problem can be solved with the information given

    d. using many different arithmetic operations to solve a problem.

Grading The Examination

The mark given a candidate is determined by comparing her results with those attained by a very large group of high school seniors. Consequently, candidates should not be discouraged by the difficulties of any of the examination items. Since almost two out of three candidates pass the examination, it is well-worth it for your students to take this test. The GED tests are designed to find out what the student knows, with less emphasis on how quickly the student can answer the questions. The student should aim at getting the highest score possible, but s/he should not feel that s/he is competing with anyone else.

Nevertheless, there are time limits on the GED tests. The allowed time is always announced at the beginning of the test so that the student can tell how much time is left. Bringing a watch can help in keeping track of the time. There is usually enough time for most people to answer all the questions, but the student should learn to pace himself. Practice in preparing for the exam helps. If the student is afraid of tests, the best way to prepare and to combat fear is to take sample tests as frequently as possible.

7. ARITHMETIC

Although your major efforts are directed at improving the communication skills of your student, s/he may consult you about her arithmetic. S/he may feel the need for some help with her homework, or s/he may have a serious problem in arithmetic. It is sometimes advantageous to devote part of the lesson to arithmetic work.

Part **4**

Additional Aids

WHAT TO DO ABOUT COMMON READING ERRORS AND DIFFICULTIES

*If your student is confused as to the side of the page on which to start reading,** s/he needs practice in building the habit of reading from left to right. Check to see if the student consistently knows the difference between his left and right side. If s/he is hesitant or unsure, s/he must first be taught this. Putting a watch, a loose rubber band, or a bracelet of any kind on his right hand will help. Play "Simon Says" with him, making the instructions very simple: Touch your right eye, your left ear, etc. If s/he makes errors, demonstrate the correct response as you give the instructions. Stand or sit beside him, not facing him, when you demonstrate to him; in this way, your left hand will be at his left. If you face him, s/he may become more confused.

After s/he has learned left from right, s/he must be given a great deal of practice in moving his eyes from left to right on the printed page. A crayoned line drawn down the left side of the page will help remind him that s/he must start to read on that side. An arrow drawn across the page from left to right will help, as will underlining the first letter. Printing the first letter of each word in colored crayon will remind him to sound out from left to right. You will find additional exercises in early grade workbooks.

*If your student has difficulty in learning the letter shapes,** remember to use all of his senses in teaching him. This is a common difficulty for young learners who have never advanced beyond the primer or pre-primer level, no matter what grade they are now in. Use cut-out letters. Have the student touch them, or trace them with his fingers, or both. Use different materials for the cut-out letters, such as felt, sandpaper, and velvet. Have him trace them in different textures. Have him shape them out of clay, out of pipe cleaners. Have him combine the letters into words, and say the words. See page 142.

Tracing the solid letters and then the outline letters will help the student learn the letter shapes.

b b b b b

b b b b b

b b b b b

b b b b b

b b b b b

b b b b b

*If your student reverses words or letters, or reads them in backwards, s/he is actually failing to read from left to right. This is so common a problem among backward readers that it requires special attention. Patient practice in sounding out letters in sequence from left to right will usually solve this difficulty. Words most frequently reversed are: **saw, was, on, no not, ton, pot, top, now, won.**

*If your student guesses and substitutes words, s/he may be reading material that is too difficult for him. Give him easier material to read. Although s/he will probably still guess, the guesses and substitutions will be fewer. Be patient; stop him, and urge him to sound out his words; however, try not to stop him too frequently. On occasion, when the substitution does not substantially alter the meaning of the material, it may be overlooked in order to add fluency to the reading.

*If your student omits words and letters, s/he is not yet reading smoothly. His eye may skip a word now and then, and s/he does not read phrases well enough to absorb the meaning of all of the words; this is also true if s/he skips letters within a word. Such errors should be called to his attention as they occur; as his skill and fluency increase, this problem should disappear. Practice in reading phrases, so that the eye takes in several words at each stop, will help in overcoming this difficulty. Suggestions for teaching the reading of phrases are on pages 148-154.

*If your student reads word by word, as though the words were in a list, s/he still finds each new word a difficult problem and is not yet able to read phrases, nor to comprehend easily what s/he is reading. The mechanics of reading are still a problem to him. This student needs practice in reading phrases and in reading with expression. The teacher should expose one phrase at a time in the reading matter so that the student is encouraged to read the whole phrase, and then move on to the next. Most important is to give the student confidence m his ability to read, to give him practice in oral reading, and to help him relax. With increased skill and relaxation, the oral reading will become expressive and less mechanical. It is also helpful to have this student read interesting books and stories that are easy, that is, at a lower reading level. Often the student can read such material fluently, and understand and enjoy it as well. Encourage him to do so. He will become confident and progress to more difficult material after a while.

*If, during silent reading, your student forms the word with his lips, s/he will have difficulty learning to read quickly. Explain to him that s/he must not say the words when s/he is reading them. Let him hold a pencil in his mouth while reading silently, to prevent the lip motion.

*If your student repeatedly loses his place while reading, let him hold a ruler or a piece of paper under the line s/he is reading. After a while, try removing it. If s/he still loses his place, let him continue the use of the line guide. Remove it when s/he no longer needs it.

*If your student confuses letters, such as, **b—d; p—q; t—f—l; m—w; u—n; h—n**; point out the slight differences between the pairs. In most cases, s/he is confusing letters that have the same shape, but face in different directions. In other cases (as **h** and **n**) the differences between the shapes of the two letters is very slight.

*In the case of letters that have the same shapes, as b and d, and p and q, the letters should be printed large, and traced. The direction in which each points should be emphasized. Try to give concrete associations to the shape of each letter. For example, **b** and **d** have flagpoles, while **p** and **q** have long tails; **b** has a big belly; **d** is a doll or a duck; **p** is like pulling a church bell down; **m** has two mountains. Associate key words with each letter. Make use, too, of the sensory aids suggested in the section on learning letters.

Exercises like the following are helpful. Have the student circle every **b**:

```
d  d  b  b  d  b  d  d  b  b  b  d  d  d

b  b  b  d  b  d  b  d  b  b  b  d  d  b

d  b  d  d  d  b  b  b  d  d  b  d  b  d

b  b  d  d  d  d  b  b  d  b  d  b  d  b

d  d  d  d  b  b  b  d  b  b  d  b  b  b

d  d  b  d  b  d  b  d  d  d  b  b  d  b

d  b  b  d  d  b  d  b  d  b  d  d  d  b

d  b  b  d  b  d  d  b  b  b  d  d  d  d

d  d  b  d  b  d  b  d  b  b  d  b  d  b
```

*If after you have pointed out the differences, s/he continues to confuse a particular pair of letters, follow this procedure: teach him one of the letters, temporarily ignoring the second. Concentrate on the first letter until s/he knows it automatically. At this point, introduce the second letter, setting aside the first one; teach the second one until s/he knows it very well. Now bring back the first, and let him work on both letters together. Though s/he may still, for a short time, confuse them slightly, s/he will quickly learn to discriminate between the two.

Sample Lesson Plan

LESSON PLAN

Student _____ Lesson _____
Teacher _____ Date _____

Goals For Today	Activites	Tutor's Comments	Next Lesson	Supervisor's Comments
1. Learn sight words	Play game Go Fish.	Went well.	Play this game again.	
2. Review sounds of short a, i	Use sound-out sheets	Needs more drill on i. Knows a	i	
3. Learn short vowel u	Use sound-out sheets	Is still hesitant.	u	
4. Develop comprehesion	Discuss TV show tutor and student saw last night	He needs encouragement to speak.	Assign same show for next week. Discuss it.	
5. Combine 1 & 4 above.	Student dictates a story for Write- Your- Own Book	Dictation went well. He cannot read many of the words.	Practice these words before trying to re-read the story.	
6. Enjoyment of reading	Read a human interest story from a news-. paper	Picked the wrong story. Not interesting to the student.	Try something related to flying. Seems interested in that.	

Above is a sample lesson plan which a tutor has prepared for his work with a student who recognizes only a few words at sight, and is learning how to sound out words. At present, this student can sound out a number of the consonant sounds, and has just learned the sounds of the short **a** and **i**. Notice that the tutor has prepared for six different activities within the one session. The lesson includes something old (review of short vowels **a** and **i**); something new (short vowel **u**); an opportunity for the student to discuss something interesting to him, thereby improving his use of spoken language. During the period when s/he dictates a story to the teacher, the student is encouraged to use his own interests as a means of developing reading matter. He is given an opportunity to relax and derive pleasure from written material, when the teacher (6) reads a very interesting brief selection to him.

The tutor has set clear and simple goals for the lesson. He is not always successful in his choice of material, or in his approach. The notes s/he makes in columns 3 and 4 are invaluable guides in remembering what should be done at the next lesson. The supervisor's comments in the last column from time to time can assist greatly in planning the tutoring.

STUDENT PROGRESS RECORD

Name _____ Tutor _____ Date _____

Date of Entry _____

	Sept.	Dec.	Mar.	June
A. Enjoys Success in Reading				
B. Understands What S/He Reads				
C. Three Major Areas of Interest				
_____				
_____				
_____				
I.. Directionality				
Knows left and right six times out of six.				
II. Word Recognition and Word Attack Skills				
1. Sight Word Vocabulary (indicate number of words the student knows)				
2. His own sight words.				
3. Gaps in phonic knowledge.				
a. Consonants:				
d, f, h, l, m, n, p, q, r, s, t, v, w, x, y, z				
b. Consonant blends:				
bl, br, pl, cl, fl, gl, sl, pr, cr, fr, gr, fr, dr,				
sp, st, sc, sk, sm, sw, sn, tw				
c. Diagraphs: sh, eh, th, ph, wh				
d. Short vowels: a, e, i, o, u				

Student Progress Sheet (continued)

    e. Long vowels: a, e, i, o, u

    f Additional vowel combinations and sounds:
      ee, ea, oo, oi, ow, ar, ir, ur, oa, ai, au, av, or,
      er, ov, ou, igh, aw,ay, ew

  4. Recognizing Prefixes and Suffixes

    a. Prefixes:
      en, ex, in, pre, con, com, de, dis, pro, re, un

    b. Suffixes:
      ing, ed, er, est, ance, ous, able, ent, ant, al,
      ive, ly, ness, ment, tion, ful

II. Common Problems

  1. Word by word reading

  2. Monotone: Lacks meaningful inflection

  3. Ignores punctuation

  4. Phrasing is poor

  5. Multisyllabic words:

    a. Compound words: reads carefully

    b. Hears the number of syllables in a word

    c. Comfortable reading new multisyllabic words

  6. Repititions

  7. Hesitations

  8. Very slow

  9. Too rapid

  10. Loses place

  11. Makes substitutions

  12. Reversals

DEVICES AND GAMES FOR TEACHING THE MECHANICS OF READING

Three by Five Cards

These are the simplest, most flexible, and most easily available of all teaching devices. They can be used:

for words to be learned, one word on a card;
for word lists;
for practice in reading a single sound, prefix, or suffix;
to encourage smoothness in reading.

For example, you might list on a card five words in which the short vowel sounds become long ones (with the addition of the final **e**). Near the edge of another small card print an **e**; Have your student place this second card so that the **e** adjoins each of the printed words in turn. Ask him to read each word with and without the final **e**.

Cards can also be used to expose individual words or phrases in order to facilitate smooth reading of textual material. Cut a rectangular slot in an unruled 3 by 5 card to form a window. Determine the size of the window by the number of words you want to expose to the student's view at one time. Slide the card across the text as the student reads.

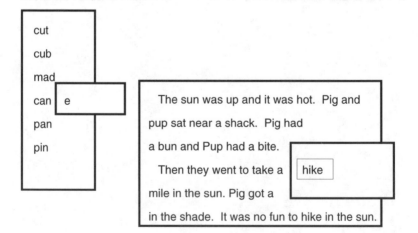

Word Wheels

Word wheels can be used to practice initial sounds, common word elements, final sounds, prefixes and suffixes. Cut two cardboard circles, one slightly smaller than the other. On the larger wheel, print the required letters. Then cut a slot in the smaller wheel, making sure that it is positioned to expose all of the words in turn as it is rotated. Place the smaller wheel on top and clip them together using a paper fastener.

Thus, for practice in the initial **br**, the upper wheel would read **br** next to the window opening. The lower wheel would show **own**, **at**, **eak**, **ush**, **ing**, **ink**, **ake**, **ain**, **ute**.

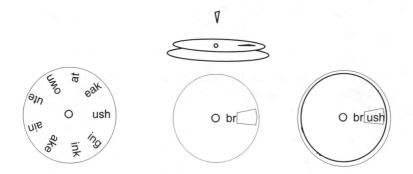

A simple type of wheel can be made of two circular pieces of cardboard, the upper one considerably smaller than the lower one. Sounds to be matched are printed next to the edge of both wheels, so that when the upper wheel is rotated, the sounds on it are matched with the word elements on the outer wheel to form new words.

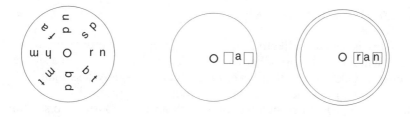

For drill in the use of prefixes and suffixes, a wheel such as shown before can be used. Note that the upper wheel shows a prefix (or a suffix) which appears beside a word-long opening. When the lower wheel

(b) is rotated, different base words appear in the opening. These can be read in combination with the prefix (or suffix).

Practice short vowels using a word wheel with two small windows separated by the vowel which is printed on the upper wheel. Appropriate consonants are arranged on the lower wheel so as to form words as the upper wheel is turned.

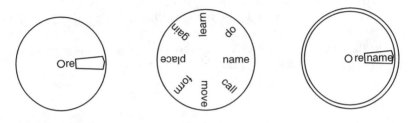

A wheel with pointers attached with a paper fastener can be used to give the student practice in adding prefixes or suffixes to the words on the wheel.

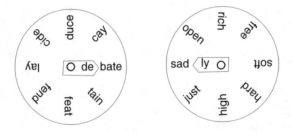

Tachistoscope

This is another effective device for practicing word recognition. Cut a window in a strip of cardboard wide enough to fold into a sleeve 4 inches wide. On another sheet of cardboard, slightly less than four inches wide, print the words that the student is learning. These words should be at least three-quarters of an inch apart and positioned so that they will be exposed through the window one at a time as the inserted card is moved up or down in the sleeve.

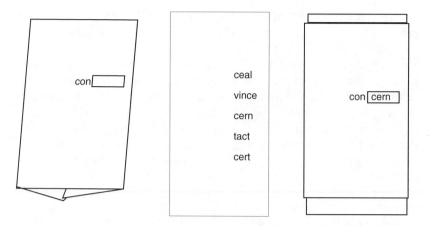

This device may be adapted for use with prefixes or suffixes. In this case, the prefix or suffix is printed on the sleeve next to the window. The base words are printed on the under sheet and exposed one at a time, allowing the student to read with the prefix or suffix added.

Television

In the center of a piece of stiff cardboard, cut two horizontal slits about two inches apart. These slits should be one quarter of an inch from top to bottom and wide enough to permit a two inch strip of paper to slide through. Adding machine paper is especially suitable for this size opening.

The roll of paper that will pass through the slits should show short printed phrases that tell a story. The paper is pulled slowly through the slits to expose several lines at a time for the student to read. For younger children, make the opening and the paper strip larger, and illustrate the strip; let the student draw and color the cardboard. This device can be adapted to help overcome word-by-word reading. For this purpose, use a smaller opening and less space between slits, so that no more than an inch of the strip is exposed at one time. In this practice, which is to develop the ability to see as many words as possible at a single glance, only one phrase should show at a time; the phrases need not necessarily relate to each other.

Do-It-Yourself Games

1. **Dominoes** can be played with word cards instead of the usual dots. The student must match words instead of dots. This will provide practice in reading and matching words, as well as in discrimination between words that s/he may substitute for each other.

		cat	run
no	no	cat	
on			

2. **Making small words out of larger ones**: Have the student make as many words as s/he can out of the letters in large words, such as **government**: **go, me, govern, men, never, ever, even, ten, move, rent, grove, vent, over, trove, rove**, and more.

3. **Decoding**: Write simple sentences or stories for the student, omitting the vowels. Have the student complete the sentences: **Wh-n w-nt-r c-m-s, c-n spr-ng b- f-r b-h-nd**?

4. **Rhymers.** Encourage the student to think of words that rhyme.

Prepare a set of puzzles similar to the following:

Think of **rode**.
    heavy_____
    like a frog_____
    the lawn was_____
    the seamstress_____

Think of **fate**.
    At lunch she_____
    The fence had a_____
    The captain had a_____
    Tardy means_____
    Fish bite at_____

5. **Editing.** Have the student rewrite your stories, making corrections. In some, prepare silly errors. In others, have the student practice punctuation. For example, have the student write this story again. Tell him to put in 7 periods and 7 capital letters that are missing.

Ellen ran to school she went to the class the teacher was in the room the boys and girls were in their seats a cat was in the room it had no seat the teacher took lunch money from everyone the cat had no lunch money.

6. **Hidden Words**. Find the hidden words. Look for words, moving from left to right or from top to bottom. When you find a word, put an outline around it, and write it at the side of the page. Can you find nine words?

7. **Buried Sentence.** Move according to directions, and find the hidden sentence.

s	m	l	T	a	j	z	w
a	t	o	h	e	e	l	x
c	a	n	t	h	p	e	t
a	t	b	e	e	h	a	n

a. Start with T, down, right T _ _
b. Start with e, right, down, left, down, right, right, up.
c. Start with s, down, right. s _ _
d. Start with o, down. o _
e. Start with t, right, down. t _ _
f. Start with c, right, up. c _ _

T _ _ e _ _ _ _ _ _ _ s _ _ o _ t _ _ c__.

8. **Bingo.** Use five-column Bingo cards. These may be used to learn letters, to learn vowels, sight words, number facts, geography facts, or any area in which the student needs practice.

Set up the Bingo cards with letters—or words—or names of cities, etc.,—and call out the matching question. In some cases, you may wish to use flash cards instead of calling out. The player uses a marker (a piece of paper, or a penny or some similar item) on the Bingo square with the correct answer. The player achieves BINGO with five markers in a row in any direction.

9. **Tic-Tac-Toe.** Instead of using X and 0 as in the traditional game of tic-tac-toe, it is fun to play it with words or letters that need practice. Each player uses one word (or letter), and the winner is the first one to complete a row, horizontal, vertical or diagonal.

10. **Anagrams, Charades, Ghost, Geography, Lotto, Map Games,** and **Quiz Games** are some common games that can very easily be adapted for reading instruction.

HELPFUL WORD LISTS

These word lists may be used in a number of ways to provide practice in teaching how to sound out words. Several suggestions follow.

1. Present the lists to your student directly from this manual. In order to show the student only one word at a time, cut a small window out of an index card and frame the word in this space.

2. Rewrite the words, as you need them, on index cards or on cardboard sheets. Use a felt-tipped pen; make each word large and clear, leaving space between the lines so that each word stands out clearly.

3. If you write each word on a separate card, the words may be used as flash cards. Be careful to present them to the student slowly at first.

4. Word wheels and other devices help to vary your presentations and add interest and novelty to the instruction (see pages 148-154).

5. Present the words in varied order, to be certain that the student recognizes each word, regardless of the order.

6. Remember that the student needs a great deal of practice. If necessary, find more words.

ALPHABET KEY WORDS

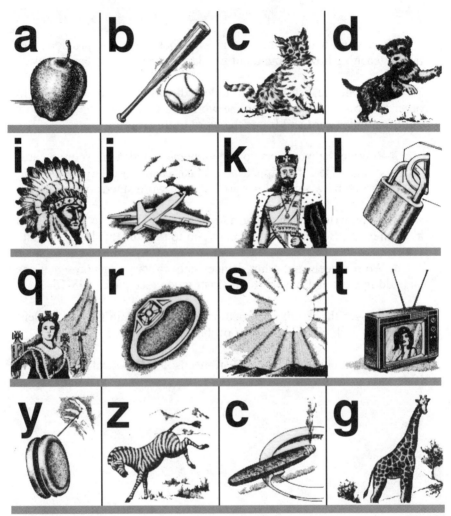

Examples of the Same Letter in Different Typefaces

Manuscript - small letters	a	b	c	d	e	f	g	h	i	j
Roman - small letters	a	b	c	d	e	f	g	h	i	j
Manuscript - capital letters	A	B	C	D	E	F	G	H	I	J
Roman - small letters	A	B	C	D	E	F	G	H	I	J

e	f	g	h
m	n	o	p
u	v	w	x
ch	sh	th	wh

k l m n o p q r s t u v w x y z

k l m n o p q r s t u v w x y z

K L M N O P Q R S T U V W X Y Z

K L M N O P Q R S T U V W X Y Z

Short Vowels

Short **a**

sat	pan	can	an	ran
ban	bat	ram	mad	bag
pat	sap	man	Sam	tap
bad	am	map	sad	cab
mat	dad	had	lad	jab
ham	ran	tan	pad	jam
fat	rag	dam	rap	tag
sag	hat	fan	has	fad
pal	lap	add	at	gap

Short **i**

is	rid	it	sit	wit	win
hip	hid	rib	fit	dig	rip
his	him	did	hit	dip	fig
tin	sill	lid	fib	wig	dim
bill	rim	nip	tip	bid	bib
sip	in	big	sin	till	fin
tip	miss	ill	bit	mill	jig

Review of Short Vowels **a** and **i**

mill	pan	dad	hid	pin	nap
rib	kit	pat	till	dim	ham
him	ran	bad	tap	had	fit
map	kill	hip	ran	rap	did
hit	bat	am	sin	bat	bib
lip	fat	lid	fib	will	dam

Short **u**

hub	but	us	hum	nut	fun
hut	rub	pup	dug	up	rug
sun	bud	mud	gum	nun	sup
bun	cub	tub	hub	rum	gun
jut	tug	bug	cud	bum	cut
run	bus	sub	rut	sum	hug

Review of Short a, i and u

sun	mill	mud	fat	bad	rut
rib	bud	pan	kid	rub	hid
till	map	bun	hut	ran	win
run	fib	sin	us	dim	cub
had	lug	rap	did	sup	bun
bib	hub	dam	tub	bus	ran

Short e

red	men	mess	bed	fez	wed
net	pet	get	well	peg	less
den	jet	bet	Ben	Tess	vet
hen	wet	bell	let	fed	tell
led	keg	hem	pen	hep	set
ten	beg	Ned	fell	met	Meg
set	pep	Ted	sex	sell	leg

Review of Short Vowels a, i, u, and e

fell	ban	dug	less	kiss	den	den
tell	hut	tub	hub	kid	tap	kill
ten	pet	dim	bun	sun	tag	had
bid	led	pen	mud	till	rib	sit
let	but	fed	sub	mill	bat	Ben

Short o

odd	hop	dot	lot	doll	rob
mob	hot	cob	hop	fog	top
pot	rot	job	not	cot	lop
nod	Tom	fob	pop	bob	sop
pod	sob	mop	cod	got	mod
rod	hod	sod	mom	tot	hog

Review of All Short Vowel Sounds

jam	get	will	rod
red	is	mob	sun
fin	add	wet	rot
jet	pot	run	mud
not	rob	sob	web
bud	bus	bad	dog
rat	bet	hot	jut
his	tap	hen	pup
lip	sin	well	man
pet	us	bed	tin
hut	bid	win	pan
web	bat	sap	pod
tub	hum	hip	sod
fan	mad	bun	dad
top	net	tip	bill

Consonants

c as in

cap	cod	can	cat
cub	cud	cuff	cot

c as in

cigar	center	cell	civil	cement
cent	cigarette	city	cellar	cereal

g as in

goat	go	gob	gal	gap
gut	got	gag	gum	girl

g as in

giraffe	gee	ginger	George	gender
gem	gin	gentle	general	giant

q as in

queen	quill	queer	quack	quarter
quit	quiz	quip	quick	question

y as in

yo-yo	yet	yap	yak	yard	your
yellow	yam	yes	yell	year	you

Long Sounds of Vowels

RULE: *When you see "o" at the end of a word, the "o" has a long sound.*

o

no	so	go	ho	yo-yo

ee

deep	feel	peep	beet	deem	beef	weep
deer	see	keel	heed	reel	fee	jeer
need	meek	deep	feet	seed	weed	leek
peel	reel	keep	reed	heel	week	keen
lee	seen	feed	seem	wee	reef	bee

ay

say	bay	hay	way	may	nay	lay
jay	day	ray	pay	gay	play	stay

ai

nail	pail	vain	bail	lair	hair	wait
main	gait	bait	mail	maid	hail	pair
lain	tail	raid	gain	paid	rail	jail
fail	fain	pain	fair	sail	maim	wail
rail	gain	wait	bait	lair	waif	aim

Double Vowels

ea

beat	neat	bead	tea	veal	peak	meal
team	hear	bean	mean	beak	heal	wean
meat	eat	ear	seal	read	leaf	meal
deal	leak	leap	real	near	seam	fear

oa

oat	load	roam	foam	goad	oak	road
goat	boat	road	coat	load	soap	oaf
goal	foal	toad	loaf	moan	soak	oar
coal	loan	hoax	moal	coax	roan	loam

ie

lie	pie	die	tie	lied	tried	cried

ue

hue	sue	rue	due	true	blue	clue

oe

doe	foe	Joe	Poe	toe	woe

Double Vowels (Mixed)

nail	wait	sue	suit	seen	hue	wheel
meat	deal	aim	sea	soap	mail	load
oak	due	leaf	pie	neat	week	beat
need	deep	feet	eat	foe	hear	teem
team	chair	foam	roar	died	tie	leak

The Silent "e"

RULE: *When you see a vowel-consonant-final "e" combination, name the first vowel and skip the "e". The final "e" is silent.*

make	mine	ate	sale	file	pure	mile
zone	line	made	cure	mate	cut	lake
bode	lane	hole	male	rave	fine	kite
tube	cake	one	life	page	use	ripe
pole	bite	time	mole	cape	rise	nine
dote	dine	sole	same	bale	mice	cope
poke	pale	fuse	five	race	dome	bake
ride	mane	date	coke	vine	like	dive
pine	cane	tune	tide	hate	rope	gale

Review of Short and Long Vowel Sounds

ripe	hop	fin	set	met	ran	goat
pad	hate	paid	bean	pine	not	tape
ruse	men	rob	neat	cub	rod	bed
bet	did	rode	can	pin	rid	tube
got	gape	mean	rip	lad	rain	died
pain	cane	dim	hat	mad	dime	tub
beat	pan	cute	rate	made	ate	cube
win	us	bait	robe	man	wine	meat
pet	rat	hope	laid	pane	road	cut

Consonant Combinations

pl	cl	bl	fl	gl
play	clock	blue	flee	glue
plow	claim	blade	flame	glass
plan	club	bless	flag	glee
plight	clang	bluff	flit	gleam
plea	clean	blank	fleet	glow
plume	clip	blink	flea	gloom
plank	clap	black	flute	glide
plain	clot	bleat	fled	glen
plane	clean	blond	flour	glean
plate	clear	bled	flog	glib
plait	clash	bleed	flog	glib
plant	clay	blood	flight	glint
plot	clam	blend	flare	glimmer
please	Clark	blare	fly	glove
plum	clerk	blunt	flask	glaze
pluck	click	blurt	flirt	glare
pleat	claw	block	fling	glad
ply	clod	blind	flint	glade
plod	clump	blame	flesh	
	clove	blame	flash	
		bleak		
		blade		

More Consonant Combinations

sl	pr	cr	fr	br
slide	print	cram	fresh	bred
slave	proof	cream	friend	bread
slid	prove	crib	frank	braid
slope	pride	crane	from	broke
slap	prune	creep	fray	brink
sleep	preach	crack	free	brand
slept	print	crush	frame	brake
slip	prick	crop	frill	break
slay	prism	crab	fright	bring
sleet	prop	cry	fringe	brought
sleigh	prize	crisp	frog	brother
sled	price	crust	fry	bride
sleeve	press	cramp	frock	brood
sloop	prod	crag	frond	brush
slight	prim	crash	frisky	brand
slink	pram	craft	fret	breech
sloppy	pretty	crazy	freak	branch
slur	proud	crease	freeze	brunch
sling	pray	creek	frail	brick
	praise	crime	France	brown
	pry	crimp	frail	broil
			froth	brim

More Consonant Combinations

gr	tr	dr	sp	st
grand	true	drive	spell	stand
gray	tree	dress	span	still
greet	track	dream	split	stain
groan	trick	drill	spat	stone
graze	truck	drank	spill	stay
grass	truck	drunk	speak	stall
green	tram	drab	speech	stake
grief	trade	drag	spin	steak
grape	trail	drake	spine	stack
greed	tramp	drape	spark	stag
grill	trap	draw	spank	stab
gripe	trash	drawn	spunk	stage
grit	tray	dry	spade	stalk
grin	treat	drip	spawn	stem
grime	trip	drop	spent	start
grim	trill	droop	spun	stark
grab	tripe	drool	spool	star
grout	try	drove	spool	steam
grog	troop	drive	spooky	stamp
ground	trace	drag	spot	stint

More Consonant Combinations

sc	sk	sm	sw	sn
scant	skinny	small	swim	snake
scat	skate	smell	sway	sneer
scold	skin	smile	sweep	snatch
scowl	skill	smart	swell	snitch
score	ski	smack	sweet	snug
scoop	sky	smite	swoon	snow
scan	skit	smock	swing	snoop
scale	skid	smog	swank	sneak
scat	skunk	smut	swear	snide
scum	sketch	smug	sweat	snip
scar	skew	smash	swat	snap
scour	skim	smoke	sworn	snack
scarf	skip	smith	swung	snag
scare	skirt	smooth	swoop	snarl
scan	skull	smother	swift	sniff
scalp		smear		snood
scout		smudge		snort
				snore
				snub

More Consonant Combinations

tw	spl	spr	str	st
twain	split	spry	strip	fast
twine	splash	sprout	stripe	most
twist	splinter	spring	string	worst
tweet	spleen	spruce	strung	last
twig	splint	sprint	strand	feast
twin	splice	sprang	strike	boast
twill	splurge	spray	struck	toast
twice		sprite	strain	yeast
twirl		sprig	street	first
tweed		sprat	straight	burst
tweak		sprawl	strait	coast
twang		spree	strange	least
twelve			strap	blast
twenty			straw	cast
twitch			stray	mast
			streak	past
			strong	lost
			strife	lust
			stretch	must
			stroke	host

More Consonant Combinations

nk	ng	nt	nd
frank	bang	want	friend
bank	sang	bent	band
tank	sing	sent	bend
shrank	wing	lent	wind
drank	swing	gent	wand
Hank	bring	bunt	sand
plank	spring	brunt	send
prank	sprang	blunt	lend
rank	fling	plant	spend
sank	flung	pliant	blond
spank	rung	runt	stand
thank	cling	slant	strand
yank	ding	faint	brand
ink	king	count	grand
blink	sling	ant	blend
link	sting	chant	mend
pink	string	grant	spend
skunk	thing	pant	trend
spunk	wrung	hint	tend
junk		lint	blind

Additional Consonant Combinations

drive	stay	glow	fling	dress	breach
prowl	flight	sleeve	crab	blunt	tray
swim	groan	smite	plait	true	frail
skill	bring	slow	pluck	swing	spool
clash	twig	crop	grip	sneer	skirt
frock	scant	glass	trail	snack	gleam
plate	plank	blond	press	brag	drug
snake	sweep	smell	skate	still	spank
train	graze	bright	gray	free	crib
drip	scab	stand	truck	crush	bless
strike	scrub	strive	crisp	skull	tract
grasp	yelp	held	strip	brisk	cleft
milk	gulf	feast	plant	splash	shelf
dump	sprite	sprout	screech	frisk	boast
film	weld	scrap	bulb	grab	belt
cramp	trust	shrink	stress	plaint	dream
spleen	desk	twin	welt	scalp	tramp
twist	trump	flame	stand	ground	crust
stream	waist	split	blot	state	lump
tweed	blend	scum	flour	wilt	smelt
skip	sport	dream	split	slept	flake
stick	scorn	prow	swept	crime	plump

Additional Consonant Sounds

sh

ship	shod	shut	dish	shot
shoe	shin	hash	shop	rash
shelf	show	shed	shun	shell
shift	shave	shore	cash	shake

ch

chick	chip	chop	chin	chit
chug	shat	chest	much	rich
catch	hatch	scratch	pitch	hitch
pinch	patch	ranch	latch	chap

th

thimble	thank	thing	thick	thump
both	with	bath		

and

than	then	them	this	the
that				

wh

whale	which	whit	whack	whine
while	wheat	wheel	whet	what
white	whim	whiff	whip	when

Review of sh, ch, th, and wh

shell	chug	rash	shin	chop	with	both
rich	chin	shelf	chest	fish	thick	chill
shop	chum	hash	this	chin	thin	whim
whip	ship	thing	show	chap	thank	whisk
the	that	them	they	their		

Additional Vowel Sounds

oo

room	soon	roof	cool	drool	broom	food
pool	boot	spool	loop	toot	moon	tool
root	shoot	spoon	hoop	boom	loon	stool

oo

stood	foot	good	book	cook	look

oi, oy

boil	soil	join	joy	coil	boy	Roy
toil	point	toy	broil	flow	spoil	coy

ow, ou

cow	owl	plow	gown	hound	stout	now
found	down	how	fowl	round	mound	sound
ground	clown	wow	frown	sour	brow	mouth

ow

low	flow	bow	row	tow	mow	slow
glow	blow	snow	throw	know	glow	crow

aw, au

paw	saw	raw	straw	shawl	haul	jaw
Saul	crawl	claw	yawn	draw	fault	dawn
lawn	Paul	raw	maul	law	flaw	craw

Review of Additional Vowel Sounds

boot	choose	show	boon	stoop	cool	thaw
bloom	food	room	book	shoot	noise	broil
smooth	coin	look	spoil	soot	choice	ouch
grouch	cook	house	joint	loud	frown	poise
shout	mooch	jaw	glow	blouse	raw	tow

Vowels Combined with r

RULE: *Vowel sounds are different when they precede r.*

ar as in car

bar	part	cart	bark	mark	car	park
hard	dark	darn	dart	charm	harm	chart
farm	lark	tar	jar	man	barb	barn
lard	tart	yarn	start	yard	march	far

or as in horse

sort	sport	fork	corn	nor	snort	cork
cord	north	short	for	or	born	York

ir as in sir, **er** as in her, **ur** as in fur

herd	term	germ	pert	hunter	clerk	birth
curl	fir	third	fur	stir	dirt	sir
teacher	flirt	fern	burn	first	twirl	cur
girl	server	skirt	shirt	church	spur	firm
turn	summer	curve	bird	burr		

Words That Rhyme

all words

wall	ball	all	hall	call	stall
fall	small	tall	gall	mall	pall

ight words

right	fight	light	sight	might	tight	bright
fright	plight	night	blight	flight	slight	bight

Words That Rhyme

an	at	am	ag	ad	ap	ot
ban	bat	am	bag	add	cap	blot
can	cat	clam	brag	bad	chap	clot
fan	brat	dam	drag	cad	zap	cot
man	flat	ram	flag	dad	clap	dot
pan	slat	jam	gag	fad	gap	knot
plan	fat	ham	hag	gad	lap	got
bran	hat	tram	lag	glad	map	hot
ran	mat	slam	crag	had	nap	jot
tan	gnat	sham	nag	lad	rap	lot
van	pat	scram	rag	mad	sap	not
began	sat		sag	pad	slap	plot
Japan	rat		snag	sad	snap	pot
	vat		tag		strap	rot
			wag		tap	shot
			zigzag		trap	slot
					pap	spot
						tot
						trot
						forgot

More Words That Rhyme

ob	it	in	id	ut	un	up	ud
Bob	bit	bin	bid	mut	bun	up	bud
lob	fit	din	did	jut	shun	cup	spud
slob	hit	chin	hid	rut	fun	pup	cud
cob	kit	hin	kid	but	gun	sup	dud
job	knit	grin	lid	cut	run		mud
mob	lit	in	mid	hut	spun		Jud
rob	pit	kin	rid	nut	stun		thud
snob	quit	pin	skid	Tut	sun		
sob	sit	shin	slid	gut	begun		
blob	slit	sin					
	spit	skin					
	split	spin					
	wit	thin					
	flin	tin					
	omit	twin					
		win					
		violin					
		begin					

More Words That Rhyme

eed	et	en	ed	old	ay	
heed	bet	Ben	bed	bold	bay	play
deed	get	den	bled	cold	play	ray
seed	jet	glen	fed	told	day	say
need	let	open	fled	mold	gray	stray
creed	met	hen	led	sold	hay	fray
bleed	net	ken	red	fold	jay	way
reed	pet	men	shed	gold	lay	away
speed	set	pen	sled	hold	May	delay
feed	wet	ten	wed	scold	pay	display
	duet	when		old	fray	pray
		then				

eat		eam		eak	
beat	peat	stream	beam	weak	streak
cheat	seat	gleam	cream	beak	squeak
eat	treat	scream	dream	teak	sneak
feat	wheat	stream	ream	leak	bleak
heat	defeat	team	seam	speak	creak
meat	pleat			peak	freak
				neat	

Compound Words

(See page 71 for additional Compound Words)

baseball	airport	tonight	moonlight
bookcase	manpower	forecast	highway
shoestring	schoolboy	milkweed	nightgown
downstairs	godfather	eyelash	understand
snowflakes	milkman	outcome	sailboat
broadcast	policeman	careless	mailman
anyone	outside	without	uptown
Sunday	inside	someone	cowhand
football	showcase	cottonseed	housefly
downtown	maybe	hallway	fullgrown
lonesome	anyway	cowboy	sunshine
peanut	bowstring	newsboy	password
schooldays	sidewalk	wallpaper	sidestep
anybody	popcorn	birthday	overcook
lighthouse	upstairs	notebook	airplane
bathroom	someday	seaman	tapdance
newspaper	midnight	grapefruit	handbag
snowball	waterfall	tablecloth	schoolroom
grandmother	godmother	within	afternoon

Practice in Syllabication

Vowel-Consonant-Consonant-Vowel Combinations

abject	aspen	cartoon	alter	expand
fourteen	bedlam	fender	benzene	blanket
expect	chimney	hostage	cancel	ignore
common	insult	butter	sudden	cordial
suffer	embed	lumber	hello	banter
cottage	traffic	correct	pencil	borrow
costume	attend	banner	barrel	hammer
awful	manner	consult	rescue	attic
plastic	walnut	magnet	cellar	postal
public	beggar	carpet	pumpkin	witness
stampede	master	sentence	margin	target
sister	summer	napkin	rabbit	kitten

Vowel-Consonant-Vowel Combinations

never	present	hotel	broken	story
caper	any	icy	ever	avoid
motel	apart	human	over	ideal
lady	direct	amount	July	August
aware	amuse	holy	female	even
lazy	crazy	tulip	before	baby
tiny	solid			

Additional Practice in Syllabication

committee	cucumber	anticipate	remember
alcohol	abdomen	aggravate	carnival
molasses	amplify	barbecue	important
innocent	entertain	occupy	February
accident	October	November	tomato
December	indirect	September	Halloween
volcano	yesterday	passenger	romantic
domestic	torpedo	carpenter	committee
remainder	surrender	rectify	republic
revolver	establish	advertise	occupant

Prefixes

Beginnings Added To Root Words

Word Wheels are helpful in learning to read these words.
(See pages149-50)

en	ex	in	pre
enter	examine	include	preschool
entire	external	insert	preview
entrance	expert	income	precede
enlist	expense	intact	precinct
enrage	expel	increase	prefer
ensue	expect	indeed	prefix
enjoy	exit	indoor	prepaid
enlarge	exist	inform	prepare
engulf	exhaust	inhale	present
engage	exhale	insane	pretend
enfold	exercise	inside	prevail
enact	excuse	insight	prevent
enable	except	inspect	prewar
endear	excite	instep	precaution
enforce	exact	insult	preside
enclose	example	intend	predict
enchant	extra	intuition	preliminary
	extreme	inland	

Prefixes

con	com	de	dis
conform	compute	deflate	disown
conceal	compound	debate	disable
convince	compose	degrade	distress
concern	complain	decay	disagree
contact	compete	deduce	dispute
concert	complete	deceive	disarm
conserve	compass	deliver	disrupt
conclude	compare	decide	disband
contract	commit	declare	discard
concrete	commerce	decline	discharge
contain	comfort	decrease	disclose
consume	comment	deduce	discount
construct	combine	defeat	discuss
consent	comic	deform	disgust
connect	comma	delay	dislike
confuse	common	demand	dismiss
		delight	distrust

Prefixes

pro	re	un
protest	redo	unsure
provoke	recall	unprepared
protect	relearn	unwashed
propose	receive	undone
pronoun	remain	unclear
promote	record	unusual
program	reduce	unhappy
profile	remove	unfold
produce	report	unfit
procure	respect	unfair
proceed	reform	uneasy
proclaim	replace	undress
proportion	retire	uncut
	reward	uncover
	regain	uncommon
	refresh	unclean
	reproduce	unborn
	resort	unarmed

Suffixes

Endings Added To Root Words

(These lists can be used in making word wheels and devices described on pages 159-165.)

s	ing	ed	er	est
helps	helping	helped	taller	tallest
asks	asking	asked	shorter	shortest
calls	calling	called	warmer	warmest
cooks	cooking	cooked	smaller	smallest
bumps	bumping	bumped	older	oldest
kicks	kicking	kicked	harder	hardest
pays	paying		newer	newest
pulls	pulling	pulled	longer	longest
starts	starting	started	lighter	lightest
thanks	thanking	thanked	kinder	kindest
wants	wanting	wanted	colder	coldest
talks	talking	talked	cleaner	cleanest
works	working	worked	blacker	blackest
adds	adding	added	sooner	soonest
burns	burning	burned	faster	fastest
barks	barking	barked	stronger	strongest
kills	killing	killed	richer	richest

farms	farming	farmed	plainer	plainest
milks	milking	milked	poorer	poorest
pants	panting	panted	nearer	nearest
stains	staining	stained	weaker	weakest
rests	resting	rested	deeper	deepest
rolls	rolling	rolled	darker	darkest
fails	failing	failed	dearer	dearest
seems	seeming	seemed	softer	softest
hears	hearing		fresher	freshest

Suffixes

ance	ous	able	ent
distance	gracious	portable	complement
clearance	infamous	probable	supplement
performance	glorious	likable	dependent
instance	poisonous	remarkable	present
ignorance	nervous	fashionable	permanent
finance	previous	enjoyable	intelligent
entrance	murderous	suitable	innocent
assistance	mountainous	desirable	incident
appearance	marvelous	dependable	resident
allowance	joyous	comfortable	excellent

al	ant	ive
mechanical	servant	extensive
practical	merchant	protective
renewal	instant	native
refusal	important	adjective
political	ignorant	locomotive
musical	distant	impressive
electrical	constant	fugitive
terminal	applicant	expensive
horizontal	accountant	selective
vertical	redundant	effective
central	pennant	destructive
carnival		captive
brutal		active

Suffixes

ly	ness	ment	tion	ful
suddenly	business	achievement	vacation	lawful
friendly	easiness	pavement	objection	skillful
sadly	lowness	movement	donation	restful
quietly	tallness	investment	destruction	powerful
gently	whiteness	shipment	exception	peaceful
justly	softness	treatment	correction	painful
yearly	highness	excitement	construction	joyful
highly	greatness	enlargement	connection	harmful
weekly	darkness	engagement	collection	handful
hardly	dampness	deportment	carnation	grateful
warmly	plainness	contentment	attraction	frightful
gladly	sweetness	betterment	adoption	faithful
sweetly	madness	assignment	ration	cupful
softly	likeness	amusement	action	bashful
freely	sadness	amazement		awful
richly	weakness	agreement		
poorly	goodness			
fairly	sickness			
deeply				
plainly				
closely				
nearly				
openly				
lovely				

MORE HELPFUL WORD LISTS

Opposites: Some Common Antonyms

sick	-	well	up	-	down
yes	-	no	boy	-	girl
walk	-	run	thin	-	fat
sit	-	stand	open	-	shut
love	-	hate	cat	-	dog
big	-	little	give	-	take
he	-	she	near	-	far
hot	-	cold	weak	-	strong
lost	-	found	wild	-	tame
light	-	dark	remember	-	forget
awake	-	asleep	happy	-	sad
before	-	after	mother	-	father
come	-	go	narrow	-	wide
black	-	white	day	-	night
noisy	-	quiet	sour	-	sweet
dead	-	alive	wet	-	dry
front	-	back	brother	-	sister
dirty	-	clean	early	-	late
empty	-	full	light	-	dark
north	-	south	off	-	on
laugh	-	cry	true	-	false
man	-	woman	strong	-	weak
top	-	bottom	in	-	out
sharp	-	dull	friend	-	enemy
young	-	old	pretty	-	ugly

Words That Sound the Same, but Are Spelled Differently and Have Different Meanings: Some Common Homonyms

buy	by	bye	be	bee
knows	nose		reed	read
sea	see		threw	through
merry	marry	Mary	male	mail
for	four	fore	new	knew
right	write		hair	hare
pane	pain		dear	deer
I	eye		beet	beat
meat	meet		add	ad
berry	bury		ale	ail
know	no		or	ore
cheep	cheap		red	read
tail	tale		gate	gait
night	knight		feet	feat
sail	sale		bow	bough
pair	pare		brake	break
bear	bare		rode	road
pail	pale		there	their
do	dew	due	week	weak
sent	scent	cent	piece	peace
so	sew	sow	ant	aunt
peek	peak		blew	blue
throne	thrown		ate	eight
to	too	two	hear	here

Words That Are Spelled Alike, but Pronounced Differently: Some Common Heteronyms

absent	congress	minute	subordinate
abuse	contact	moped	suspect
accent	convict	object	tear
address	coordinate	perfect	transplant
affiliate	deliberate	present	transport
alternate	discount	primer	triplicate
annex	duplicate	read	underestimate
approximate	estimate	rebel	upset
articulate	excuse	record	use
bow	increase	reject	wound
buffer	insert	resume	
close	intimate	sewer	
compact	invalid	sew	
compound	lead	subject	

Selected List of Words That Have Several Meanings: Homophones

about: concerning, approximately, around, ready to
act: do, pretend, law
address: speak, specific place
anxious: concerned, eager
bear: carry, animal
brand: mark (label), kind
care: to be fond of, to look after
chance: opportunity, possibility, luck
coarse: rough, common, crude
company: group, business, visitors
contract: agreement, shrink
cool: chilly, calm
date: time, appointment, fruit
digest: absorb, understand, summary
dressing: bandage, sauce
drop: fall, stop, small amount
electrify: shock, thrill
entertain: delight, consider
examine: study, test
faculty: talent, teachers
fence: railing/partition, bootleg, sword-fight
firm: solid, company
follow: trail, pursue, obey
forge: build, counterfeit, smelter, progress
freeze: chill, stiffen
grasp: hold, control, understand
grub: dig, toil, larva, food
harvest: gather, crop,

just: precisely, only, fair

list: record, slant

manual: handbook, by hand

origin: beginning, root

peer: equal, look

pool: small body of water, combine

race: hurry, group of people

responsible: accountable, trustworthy

rock: swing, stone

scrap: fight, particle, waste

spot: stain, recognize

stage: to perform, level, platform

straight: direct, honest, conventional

switch: a strap, beat, to change

tape: to record, sealing material for papers and equipment

worn: used, tired

vault: a safe, a tomb, to jump

volume: quantity, a book

watch: view, guard, instrument for telling time

Sample Comprehension Skills Exercises

Some the following sentences are true, some are false, and some are statements of opinion. Can you tell which are which?

1. Cats chase mice.
2. Most people are right handed.
3. The sun sets in the west.
4. The sky is pink.
5. All dogs have shaggy black hair.
6. A window always has two panes of glass.
7. President Reagan was the wisest president we ever had.
8. A morning cup of coffee is an excellent stimulant.
9. A cigarette a day is not harmful to health.
10. Mark Twain was a funny man.
11. Vitamin C helps avoid many illnesses.
12. This book will undoubtedly become a best-seller.
13. The giraffe has a very long neck.
14. Dogs meow.
15. The sea is salty.
16. A school contains classrooms.
17. Australia is in the southern hemisphere.
18. A magic marker is a ball point pen.
19. The sky is cloudy all the time.
20. The weather in Washington, D. C. is quite comfortable in the summer.
21. My mother is the most beautiful woman in the world.
22. Vanilla ice cream is more delicious than chocolate.
23. Down pillows are more comfortable than polyurethane.
24. Dr. Smith is a fine dentist.
25. The sun sets in the west.

26. The moon is blue.

27. A ping pong ball can be used in playing golf.

28. Canoes have sails.

29. Purple is a color.

30. Kansas City is in the United States.

Sample Sentences in which One can Find the Answers to the Questions: Who? What? When? Where? Why? How?

1. Frieda Geller sometimes worked during the morning at the clinic to help the staff by keeping attendance records of the children who came.

2. Driving down Neptune Avenue at 8:00 A. M., the policeman carefully watched for cars that might be speeding.

3. The Atlantic Ocean last year flooded the beach at Sea Gate with loud crashing waves due to a major hurricane.

4. Early in the morning Grandfather always prepared hot oat meal in the kitchen for breakfast for his grandchildren.

5. The children clapped loudly because they enjoyed today's concert and dance recital at the Brooklyn Academy of Music.

6. Early in the morning, the firemen drove out of the fire station quickly to put out the big fire.

7. To build a house, the builder uses plans drawn up by the architect in advance.

8. With the FAX machine, people can now send messages to friends and business associates all over the world instantly.

9. John watched NORTHERN EXPOSURE on his TV set Monday evening to learn about Dr. Joel's latest adventures in Cecily, Alaska.

10. The Frugal Gourmet on Channel 13 on Saturday afternoon showed how to cook a special sauce for vegetarians who can't tolerate spicy food.

11. To help make the health fair a success in May, the children painted squares for the patchwork quilt to be displayed at the table.

Part 5

Appendix: Helpful Resources

PUBLISHERS OF LITERATURE TO INSPIRE, ENCOURAGE, AND OPEN THE WORLD OF READING FOR BEGINNING AND DISABLED READERS OF ALL AGES

The number of books available for the beginning reader has sky-rocketed in recent years, particularly in the field of children's books. It is impossible to enumerate here the many excellent books that are helpful and pleasurable for the persons for whom you are providing remedial instruction. Have confidence in your own judgment of books that you find to be interesting and attractive. Your local librarian can be helpful, as can catalogues from the following publishers. Ask for catalogues of literature-based reading materials.

*Those throughout this part marked * are particularly helpful with adults and young adults.*

*Avon Books, 1350 Ave. of the Americas, New York, NY 10019
   Award winning books by notable authors for children and young adults, including a sizable list of multicultural books.

Dell Publishing Company, 666 Fifth Avenue, New York, NY 10103 800-223-6834
   YEARLING BOOKS are inexpensive paperback adaptations of children's classics, including biographies of Abraham Lincoln, Frederick Douglass and John F. Kennedy.
   Rdg. Level: 2-8; Interest Level: Children, Early Teens

*Globe Book Co./Simon and Schuster, 113 Sylvan Ave., Englewood Cliffs, NJ 07632
   AMERICAN or WORLD BIOGRAPHIES
   Biographies, with vocabulary and interpretative reading activities.

Greenwillow Books (Div. of Wm. Morrow), 1350 Ave. of the Americas, New York, NY 10019   800-631-1199

Harper-Collins Publishers, 10 East 53 St., New York, NY 10022 800-242-7737

Houghton Mifflin Publishing Company, One Beacon Street, Boston, MA 02108   800-257-9107

McGraw Hill Publishing Co., 866 Third Ave., New York, NY 10022

William Morrow and Co., 1350 Ave. of the Americas, New York, NY 10019 800-843-9389

Orchard Books (Franklin Watts), 95 Madison Ave., New York, NY 10016 800-433-3411

*Readers Digest, Pleasantville, NY 10570 800-431-1726
    Success in reading one of the Readers Digest simple books is a
    source of enormous pleasure for a beginning reader, particularly
    adult or young adult.
    GIANT STEP STORY-BOOKS are helpful with children.
    Rdg. Level: Beginning; Interest Level: Children

*Readers House, Literacy Volunteers of New York City, Publishing
Department, 121 Avenue of the Americas, New York, NY 10013
    These books are particularly useful for adult and young adult dis-
    abled readers; they are low reading level, high interest level.

Scholastic, Inc., 730 Broadway, New York NY 10003; 800-392-2179
    Inexpensive paperbacks.

Scott, Foresman and Co., 1900 E. Lake Avenue, Glenview, IL 60025
800-782-2665

Simon & Schuster, 866 Third Ave. New York, NY 10022

Viking-Penguin USA, 375 Hudson St., New York, NY 10014

ANNOTATED LIST OF PUBLISHERS OF MATERIALS THAT EMPHASIZE READING SKILLS AND VOCABULARY DEVELOPMENT

Students in remedial programs need assistance in developing specific reading skills, as outlined in the text. The publishers listed here
produce many materials that are helpful in skills development, and
many also list literature for reading for pleasure:

For All Age Levels

*Book-Lab, Inc., P.O. Box 206, Ansonia Station, New York, NY 10023   (800) 654-4081
  Fine material for ESL and for students with special needs.
  The 'Write' Way To Spell, Vol 1 & 2
  Vowels and Stories
  RECIPE FOR MATH
  HIP READER PROGRAM
  Health for Our Times
  Our Constitution; Our Government
  History of the United States, Books 1 & 2, textbooks & workbooks
  World History

*Contemporary Books, Inc., 2 Prudential Plaza (Suite 1200), Chicago, IL 60601   312-540-4500
  Number Power
  Ready, Set Study
  Bridges to Critical Thinking: Reading Non-Fiction
  BRIDGES TO CRITICAL READING: READING STORIES
    Math skills, study skills and thinking skills are dealt with in these books.
  LET'S READ TOGETHER AND STORIES FOR YOUNG PARENTS
    Paperbacks, reading level 2-3, young adult and adult interest level.

DLM, One DLM Park, Allen, TX 75002
  Multisensory and helpful instructional supportive materials.

Doubleday and Company, 666 Fifth Avenue, New York, NY 10103
  Thorndike-Barnhart High School Dictionary

Easier to Learn, Patchogue, NY 11772   516-475-7693
  GLASS ANALYSIS PROGRAM,
    A reading program that focuses on word attack via syllables.

Educators Publishing Service, 75 Moulton Street, Cambridge, MA 02138   800-225-5750
  Excellent material for remedial instruction. Their materials are a must in a remedial program. Particularly noteworthy are *Primary Phonics* and Nina Traub's *Recipe for Reading* program.

Gareth Stevens, Inc., 1555 N. River Center Dr., Suite 201,
Milwaukee, WI 53212
> OUR CENTURY 1900-1990; Nine volumes, one for each decade
> from 1900 to 1990.
>> These books use newspaper format; they promote reading news
>> papers and stimulate discussion, as well as help develop reading
>> strategies.

Fearon/Janus, 500 Harbor Blvd., Belmont, CA 94002
> WORK TALES; 10 titles dealing with problems encountered in
> the work place, with discussion questions after each chapter.
> Reading level0-4.

Instructional/Communications Technology, 10 Stepar Place,
Huntington Station, NY 11746 800-225-5428
> Use of multimedia that encourages early independent reading.
> Faithful renditions of the literary quality of children's
> literature, using the technology of the twenty-first century.

*Jamestown Publishers, Box 9168, Providence, RI 02940
800-USA-READ
> *Reading the Newspaper*
> *Beyond Basics*
> *Selections From the Black Book*
> *Selections From the Restless Book*
> *Best Selling Chapters*
> *Skimming and Scanning*
>> These books lend themselves to effective use of prereading,dur-
>> ing reading and after-reading activities; they lend themselves to
>> developing interpretive reading skills.

*New Readers Press, Publishing Division of Laubach Literacy
International 1320 Jamesville Avenue, P.O. Box 131, Syracuse, NY
13210, 800-448-8878
> Collections of stories at first and second grade reading
> levels, in addition to material on skills instruction.
> Particularly helpful with adults and young adults.
> Also *Government Today* text and workbook, and *Reading in the
> Content Areas* encourage critical analysis (reading levels 5-8);
> and *Timeless Tales* (reading levels 2-3).
> WHOLE LANGUAGE FOR ADULTS series; four titles
> *A Guide to Instruction*
> *A Guide to Portfolio Assessment*

A Guide to Initial Assessment
A Guide to Administration and Staff Development

*Phoenix Learning Resources, 2345 Chaffee Road, St. Louis, MO
63416 800-221-1274
   Good source of remedial materials.
   Helpful series:
   PROGRAMMED READING by Sullivan and Buchanan
      Rdg. Level: K-6; Interest Level K-6/ESL
   READING READINESS, by Sullivan and Buchanan
      Rdg. Level: Pre-School-1; Interest Level: Same, ESL
   PROGRAMMED READING FOR ADULTS, by Sullivan and
      Buchanan Rdg. Level: 1-6; Interest Level: 7-Adult
   NEW PRACTICE READERS, by Anderson, Stone and Dolen
      Red. Level: K-8; Interest Level: 2-Adult

*Sennet and Sarnoff Learning Systems, Inc., 20 East 49 Street, New
York, NY (212) 308-5926
   This company publishes POWERWORDS, a program for vocabulary development suitable for the student preparing for the GED
   or the SAT.

SRA (Macmillan/McGraw Hill), 155 N. Wacker Drive, Chicago,
Illinois 60606
   THE MERRILL LINGUISTIC READING PROGRAM and the
   MERRILL LINGUISTIC SKILLTEXT SERIES are basic to a
      program for disabled readers. Reading Level: Beginning to 6;
      Interest Level: All.

*Steck-Vaughn Company, Box 26015, Austin, TX 78155
800-531-5015
   In this catalogue, you will find material useful in skills instruction and in teaching critical thinking, as well as their SPOTLIGHT
   series, biographies of interest to older students at the 2-4 reading
   level: biographies of Madonna, Tom Cruise, Mike Tyson, among
   others.
   Voices: From American History
   Voices: From World History
   World History For You
      These books contain maps, photographs, graphs. Reading and
      writing activities are integrated with vocabulary development and
      critical thinking.
   Writing for Competency

*Wilson Language Training, 162 West Main Street, Millbury, MA
01527-1943 800-899-8454
 WILSON READING SYSTEM: a helpful program based on
 skills development for disabled readers; interest level fifth grade
 through adult.

THE FOLLOWING ARE PARTICULARLY HELPFUL WHEN TEACHING STUDENTS FOR WHOM ENGLISH IS A SECOND LANGUAGE OR ADULTS WITH SIGNIFICANT READING DELAY*

Addison-Wesley/Longman Publishing Group, 15 Columbus Circle,
New York, NY 10023
 In Good Company by Drayton and Skidmore
 *Reading By All Means: Reading Improvement Strategies for
 English Language Learners* by Fraida Dubin and Elite Olshtain.
 1990
 Three Easy Pieces by Fraida Dubin and Elite Olshtain, 1990

Alemany Press/Higher Ed. Division, 15 Columbus Circle, New York,
NY 10023
 Benchmark Reading by Rathmell

Book-Lab, P.O. Box 206, Ansonia Station, New York, NY 10023
800-654-4081
 The 'Write' Way To Spell, Vol 1 & 2
 Health for Our Times
 Our Constitution; Our Government
 History of the United States, Books 1 & 2, textbooks & workbooks
 World History

Cambridge Book Co./PHR, 15 Columbus Circle, New York, NY
10023
 The New Arrival Books 1 & 2, by Laurie Kuntz
 Using the Newspaper: Communication Competencies For Adults,
 by Sally Grimes Pasley and Dee Koppel Williams, 1987.

---

*I wish to thank Stephan Poppick for assistance with the bibliography for
adult and ESL students.

Collier/Macmillan, 866 Third Ave., New York, NY 10022
No Hot Water Tonight by Jean Bodman and Michael Lanzano
No Cold Water Tonight Either, by Jean Bodman and Michael Lanzano

Contemporary Books, 180 N. Michigan Ave., Chicago, IL 60601
800-691-1918
Look At the U.S. Books 1 & 2, by Sally Wigginton

Fearon Education, 500 Harbor Blvd., Belmont, CA 94002
HOPES AND DREAMS SERIES by Tara Reiff, 1989

Litmore Publishing and Delta Books/Bantam, 666 Fifth Ave., New York, NY 10103
800-223-6834
Personal Stories by Linda Mrowicki
First Words
Starting to Read

Cambridge University Press, 40 W. 20 St., New York, NY 10011
800-221-4512
Task Reading by Davis, Whitney, Pike, Baky and Blass

Lateral Communication/Longman Publishing Group: (see below)
Basics in Reading: An Introduction to American Magazines by Eleanore Boone, Joseph Bennett and Lyn Motal, 1988.

Lingual House/Longman Publishing Group: (see beelow)
First Steps in Listening by Nobuhiro Kumai and Michael Rost

Longman Publishing Group, 10 Bank St., White Plains, NY 10606
True Stories in the News by Sandra Heyer, 1987
More True Stories in the News, by Sandra Heyer, 1990
Faces in the USA, by Elizabeth Laird
The American Dream by Hocmard, Sommers, Sheram and Wolff
The Whole Story by Richard Rossner. 1988
Strategies in Reading Developing Essential Reading Skills by Lyn Motai and Eleanor Boone, 1988
Problem Solving: Critical Thinking and Communications Skills, by Linda W. Little and Ingrid Greenberg, 1991.
All About the USA, A Cultural Reader, by Milada Broukal and Peter Murphy, 1991.

New Readers Press, Laubach Literacy Int'l., Box 131, Syracuse, NY 13210
FITTING IN SERIES by Rosanne Keller. 1990
KALEIDOSCOPE SERIES by Sara Hoskinson Frommer. 1990
Remembering. Books 1 & 2 by adult students in the basic reading classes at the Lutheran Settlemen House Women's Program, Philadelphia, PA, 1988

Newbury House Publishers, Reading, MA:
Experience Reading Literature by John Dennis
Facts and Figures by Pat Ackert
Cause and Effect by Pat Ackert
English by Newspaper by Terry Frederickson and Paul Wedel
Far From Home by William Pickett
Developing Reading Skills by Markstein and Hirasawa
American Articles 1 & 2 - Reading the Culture by Tracey Ruffner
Reflections by Griffin and Dennis

Prentice Hall Regents (PRH), 113 Sylvan Ave., Englewood Cliffs, NJ 07632
Unusual Stories from Many Lands by Arlo T. Janssen
Stories from Latin America by Larry T. Myers
At the Door by McKay and Petitt
Noah and the Golden Turtle by Sarah Skinner Dunn
Time and Space by Connelly and Sims
Outsiders by Jean S. Mullen
Beyond the Beginning by Hyzer, Neidermeier and Church
Yesterday and Today in the USA by Anna Harris Live
Reading in English 1, 2 & 3 by Banks and Rowe
Variations by Patricia Duffy
Voices of Freedom, Books 1 and 2, by Bliss
EVERYTHING'S DIFFERENT SERIES, 1990

Scott Foresman and Co., 1900 E. Lake Ave., Glenview IL 60025
COMPREHENSION SERIES A-F, Adult Reading
PEOPLE, CULTURE, COPING, 2 -7 grade reading
Holidays in the USA: An ESL Reader by Catherine Porter, Elizabeth Minicz and Corde Cross, 1991
This Land Is Your Land

Steck-Vaughn, Box 26015, Austin, TX 78755   800-531-5015
WONDERS OF SCIENCE SERIES, 2-3 grade reading level
Amnesty—A Real Life Approach

IF YOU WANT TO LOOK FURTHER FOR BOOKS ON YOUR OWN; Bibliographies Of Books Useful in Reading Programs

American Indian Reference Book For Children and Young Adults, collected by Barbara J. Kuipers, Libraries Unlimited, Englewood, CO, 1991

The Best Years of Their Lives, Stephanie Zvirin, Chicago, American Library Association, 1992.
A bibliography of books of interest to teenagers, dealing with crises and problem areas.

Black Authors and Illustrators of Children's Books, 2nd Ed., Barbara Rollock, NY, Garland, 1992.
Biographical Dictionary and Bibliography

Easy Reading: Book Series and Periodicals for Less Able Readers (2nd Edition), by Randall J. Ryder, Bonnie B. Graves and Michael F. Graves, Newark, DE, International Reading Association, 1989

"For Adults Only: Reading Materials for Adult Literacy Students," F. E. Kazemak and P. Riggs, *Journal of Reading*, 28, pps.726-31, 1985

A Guide to Juvenile Books About Hispanic Peoples and Cultures by Isabel Scion, Scare Crow Press, Div. of Grolier, Inc., Shermans Tpke., Danbury, CT 06816

Human and Anit-Human Values in Children's Books, Interracial Books for Children, 1841 Broadway, New York, NY 10023, 1976.
This book is now out of print, but it may be available in libraries.

Kaleidoscope: A Multicultural Booklist for Grades K-8, Rudine Simms Bishop, Ed., National Council of Teachers of English, Urbana, IL, 1994

Our Family, Our Friends and Our World: An Annotated Guide to Multicultural Books for Children and Teenagers, Lyn Miller-Lachmann, R. R. Bowker, NY, 1992

Japanese Children's Books, 1972
Light and Candles: The Jewish Experience in Children's Books, 1993
The Black Experience in Children's Books, 1989.
Published by the New York Public Library, Fifth Avenue at 42nd Street, New York, NY 10018

Multicultural Publishers Exchange Catalog of Books By and About People of Color, The Highsmith Co., Inc., W5527 Highway 106, P.O. Box 800, Ft. Atkinson, Wisconsin 53538; 800-558-2110

Paperback Books for Children: A Selected List Through Age Thirteen, Bank Street College, New York, NY, 1988

"Resources to Identify Children's Books," Arlene M. Pillar, in *Invitiation to Read,* Bernice E. Cullinan (Ed.), Newark, DE, International Reading Association, 1992

This Land is Our Land: A Guide to Multicultural Literature for Children and Young Adults, Aletha K. Helbig and Agnes B. Perkins, 1994, Greenwood Press, Wesport, CT

PUBLISHERS AND MANUFACTURERS OF GAMES THAT ARE USEFUL IN READING PROGRAMS

Home-made games are inexpensive, fun to make, fun to use, and very helpful in instruction. Many commercial games can easily be adapted for instructional use. The following are only a few of the manufacturers of games that you may find useful. In addition to the following, many book publishers also produce games:

Milton Bradley Company, P.O. Box 3400, Springfield, MA 01101

Beckley-Cardy Company, 92 Madison Ave., Montgomery, NY 12549

Cardinal Industries, 201 51 Avenue, Long Island City, NY 11101
    Basic games such as Chess, Checkers, Bingo, Dominoes, Board Games

Childcraft, 20 Kilmer Rd., Edison, NJ 08818

Constructive Playthings, 1227 E. 119 St., Grandview, MO 64030

Discovery Toys, Phyllis Pratt, 207-05 Hillside Avenue, Queens Village, NY 11427 718-465-1266

Hoiland Publication, Inc. Box 31130 Bloomington, MN 55431 800-541-9588

New Directions Press, R.D. 4, Box 4144, Newton, NJ 07850
    Pope-Dinola Word Bank

Parker Brothers, 50 Dunham Rd., Beverly, MA 01915

Pressman Toy Co., 200 Fifth Avenue, New York, NY
    Wordsearch and Wheel of Fortune (like Hangman)

INSTRUCTIONAL COMPUTER SOFTWARE: PUBLIC DOMAIN AND SHAREWARE

See page 211. Although computer softwear is usually quite costly, there are several sources for inexpensive softwear. The following companies list many instructional materials and games for less than $5 per disk; the programs on these disks are either in the public domain (which means that they are not copyrighted and may be used by anyone) or are "shareware." Authors of shareware permit purchasers to try their programs; if they like them and wish to take full advantage of them, users are requested to register with the author and pay a modest fee in addition to the initial purchase price. This is a useful way to try programs that may be useful and enjoyable.

The M & M Software Library, P.O. Box 15795,Long Beach, CA 90815 800-642-6163

Reasonable Solutions, 1221 Disk Dr. Medford, OR 97501 800-876-3475

INSTRUCTIONAL COMPUTER SOFTWARE: COMMERCIAL

Broderbund Software, PO Box 6125, Novato, CA 94948-6125, 800 521-6263

Davidson & Associates, Inc., PO Box 2961, Torrance, CA 90509, 800 545-7677

Discus Knowledge Research, Inc., 45 Sheppard Ave East, Suite 410, Toronto, ON M2N5W9, CANADA, 800 567-4321

Edmark Corp., PO Box 3218, Redmond, WA, 800 362-2890

Educational Activities, P.O. Box 392, Freeport, NY 11520, 800-645-3739
    Videos, software, multimedia, early childhood through adult

Hartley Courseware, 3001 Coolige Rd., Suite 400, East Lansing, MI 48823, 800 247-1380

Jostens Learning Corp., 7878 N. 16th St., Suite 100, Phoenix, AZ 85020, 800 422-4339

The Learning Company, 6493 Kaiser Dr., Fremont, CA 94555, 800 852-2255

MECC, 6160 Summit Dr. North, Minneapolis, MN 55430-4003, 800 685-6322

Microsoft Corp., One Microsoft Way, Redmond, CA 98052, 800 426-9400

National Geographic Society, 1145 17th St. N.W., Washington, DC 20036, 800 368-2728

Tom Snyder Productions, 800 Coolige Hill Rd., Watertown, MA. 800 342-0236

The Voyager Company, 1 Bridge St., Irvington, NY 10533, 800 446-2001

MULTIMEDIA

Instructional/Communications Technology, Inc. (ITC) 10 Stepar
Place, Huntington Station, NY 11746 800 225-5428
> *Look, Listen and Learn,* a Multimodal Multimedia System for
> Beginning Readers. Use of multimedia that encourages early
> independent reading. Programs develop faithful renditions of
> the literary quality of children's literature, using the technolo-
> gy of the 21st Century. Send for their catalog.

PERIODICALS OF INTEREST TO YOU AND YOUR STUDENTS

For All Ages:

National Geographic Magazine, 17th and M Sts. NW., Washington,
D.C. 20036

Natural History, American Museum of Natural History, 79 St. and
Central Park West, New York, NY 10024

Popular Mechanics, The Hearst Corp. Box 10069, Des Moines, IA
50350

Popular Science, Times Mirror Magazines, Box 2871 Boulder, CO
80302

Local newspapers
 and

Black Enterprise, Graves Pub. Co., 130 5th Ave. New York, NY
10011

Consumer Reports, Consumers Union, 256 Washington St. Mt.
Vernon, NY 10533

Ebony, Box 690, Chicago, IL 60605

Ebony Man, Johnson Pub. Co., 820 S. Michigan Ave., Chicago, IL
60605

Essence, Box 51300, Boulder, CO 80321

Family Circle, Box 3156, Harlan, IA 51593

Hispanic Magazine, Hispanic Pub. Corp., 111 Massachusetts Ave.
N.W., Washington, DC 20001

MS, Box 57122, Boulder, CO 80321

Newsweek, The Newsweek Bldg., Livingston, NJ 07039

Parents, Box 3055, Harlan, IA 51593

Readers Digest, Pleasantville, NY 10570

Sassy, Lang Communication, 230 Park Ave., New York, NY 10169

Time, 541 N. Fairbanks Court, Chicago, IL 606611

For Grade School Children:

Boy's Life, Boy Scouts of America, Box 152079, 1325 W. Walnut Hill Lane, Irving, TX 75015

Cobblestones, Cobblestone Publishing, Inc. 30 Grove Street, Peterborough, NH 03458

Cricket, Carus Corp., 315 5th Street, Peru, IL 61354

Dolphin Log, The Cousteau Society, Inc. 8440 Santa Monica Blvd., Los Angeles, CA 90069

Electric Company Magazine, 1 Lincoln Plaza, New York NY 10023

Kids, Time Inc. Magazine Co., Time and Life Building, Rockefeller Center, New York, NY 10020

Highlights for Children, 803 Church Street, Honesdale, PA 18431

News for You, New Readers Press, Laubach Literacy.
Weekly newspaper in 2 levels of difficulty; especially useful to young adult and adult readers. Levels 3-4 and 5-6

Ranger Rick, National Wildlife Federation, 8925 Leesburg Pike, Vienna VA 22184.

Scope, Scholastic Magazines, 730 Broadway, New York, NY 10003

Starting Point, Rolo Publishing Co., 8568 S.W. 113th, Miami, FL 33173. 800 654-4081
Content-based, whole language magazine for Middle and High School students reading at 3 to 4 grade level.

Sports Illustrated for Kids, Time Magazine Co., Rockerfeller Center, New York, NY 10020

*U*S* Kids.* Children's Better Health Institute, 1100 Waterway Blvd., Indianapolis, IN 46202

Zillions, Consumers Union of US Inc., 256 Washington St., Mt. Vernon, NY 10553

Weekly Reader Publications: The Weekly Reader Corp., 245 Long Hill Rd., PO Box 2791, Middletown, CT 06457

*Know Your World Extra**
Reading level 2-3

*Current Events**
Bi-weekly; middle school level

*Current Science**
Sept.-May. Bi-weekly newspapers in two levels of difficulty (for slow readers of all ages)

*Read Magazine**

*Weekly Reader**
Weekly newspaper in levels Pre-K to 6

BACKGROUND READING FOR THE TUTOR

Primer For Parents, Paul McKee, Houghton-Mifflin Co., 1966

Teacher, Sylvia Ashton-Warner, Simon and Schuster, Inc. (or Bantam Paperback), 1963

Guidelines To Teaching Children With Learning Problems, Lillie Pope, New York, Book Lab, 1986

Teacher's Sampler, L. Pope, D. Edel and A. Haklay, New York, Book-Lab, 1978

Special Needs: Special Answers, L. Pope, D. Edel and A. Haklay, New York, Book-Lab, 1976

Coping With Kids and School, Linda Albert, E. P. Dutton, New York, 1985
Questions and answers on school-related problems

Choosing Books For Children: A Common Sense Guide, Betsy Hearne, New York, Dell, 1982
How to select different types of books, with recommendations.

The Reading-Aloud Handbook, Jim Trelease, New York, Penguin Books, 1985.
The hows and whys of reading aloud, together with read aloud selections.

All Speed Out, Betsy Rubin, Chicago, Contemporary Books, Inc. 1986

Solving Language Difficulties, Nina Traub and Frances Bloom, Cambridge, Educators' Publishing Service, 1975

Facts and Fiction: Literature Across the Curriculum, Bernice E. Cullinan, Newark, DE, International Reading Association, 1993.

Illiteracy, A National Dilemma, D. Harman, New York, Cambridge Adult Book Company, 1987

The Complete Theory to Practice Handbook of Adult Literacy: Curriculum Design and Teaching Approach, Rena Soifer et al., New York, Teachers College Press, 1990

Teaching Adults to Write, a Brief Guide for the Teaching of Writing, Scott Foresman and Co., 1986

The Art of Teaching Writing, by Lucy McCormick Calkins, Heinemann, 1986.

OF SPECIAL INTEREST TO THOSE WHO TEACH ENGLISH AS A SECOND LANGUAGE

Whole Language for Second Language Learners, Y.S. Freeman and D. E. Freeman, Portsmouth, NH, Heinemann, 1992

The Natural Approach, S.D. Krashen and T. D. Terrell, Englewood Cliffs, NJ, Alemany Press/Prentice Hall, 1983

Caring and Sharing in the Foreign Language Class: A Sourcebook on Humanistic Techniques. G. Moskowitz, Cambridge, MA, Newbury House, 1978

Bringing Literacy to Life Issues and *Options in Adult ESL Literacy*, H.S. Wrigley and G.J.A. Guth, San Mateo, CA, Laguirre, Int'l, 1992

PERIODICALS OF INTEREST TO THE TUTOR

Academic Therapy, 1539 Fourth Street, San Rafael, CA 94901

Day Care and *Early Education*, Behavioral Publications, 72 Fifth Avenue, New York, NY 10011

Early Years, Allen Raymond, Inc., Hale Lane, Darien, Conn. 06820

Instructor, Scholastic Inc., P.O. Box 53896, Boulder, CO 80322 800-544-2917

Learning, 1111 Bethlehem Pike, P.O. Box 908, Springhouse, PA 19477

Teacher, Macmillan Professional Magazines, Inc. 22 West Putnam Ave., Greenwich, CT 06830

Teaching K-8, Box 54808, Boulder, CO 80322   800-678-8793

SPECIAL INTEREST ASSOCIATIONS, LISTED WITH NEWSLETTERS PUBLISHED BY SOME OF THEM

Amer. Assoc. for Adult and Continuing Education (AAACE), 1201 Sixteenth St. (Suite 230), Washington, DC 20036
   Adult Learning

American Library Association, 50 East Huron Street., Chicago, Illinois 60611

Children with Attention Deficit Disorders (CHADD), 499 Northwest Avenue, Suite 308 Plantation, FL 33317
   The C.H.A.D.D.ER Box

Council on Adult Basic Education (COABE), For information: Stan Brown, Newport Public Schools, 437 Broadway, Newport, RI 02840
   Adult Basic Education

Council for Exceptional Children (CEC), 1920 Association Drive., Reston, VA 22091 800-845-6232

International Reading Association (IRA), 800 Barksdale Rd., P.O. Box 8139, Newark, DE 19714
   Journal of Reading, Reading Teacher, Reading Today

Laubach Literacy International, 1320 Jamesville Avenue., Box 131, Syracuse, NY 13210

Literacy Assistance Center, Inc. , 15 Dutch St., 4th Fl., New York NY 10038
   Literacy Update

Learning Disabilities Association (LDA), 4156 Library Rd., Pittsburgh, PA 15234

Literacy Volunteers of America, 5795 Widewaters Parkway, Syracuse, NY 13214

National Council of Teachers of English (NCTE), 1111 Kenyon Rd., Urbana, IL 61801

National Education Association (NEA), 1201 16 Street, N.W., Washington, DC 20036

Orton Dyslexia Society, Chester Bldg., Suite832, 8600 LaSalle Rd., Baltimore, MD 21286
   Perspectives

Reading is Fundamental, Inc., Publications Dept., 600 Maryland Avenue S.W.,Washington, DC 20024

Teachers of English for Speakers of Other Languages (TESOL) 1600 Cameron St. (Suite 300), Alexandria, VA 22314
   Tesol Matters and *Adult Education* Newsletter

United Federation of Teachers (UFT), 260 Park Avenue South, New York, NY 10003

GLOSSARY

accent: the stress given to a syllable so that it will be more prominent than other syllables; a characteristic pronunciation influenced by the speaker's native language or regional background.

affix: a prefix or suffix.

antonym: words having opposite meanings, such as up/down.

articulation: (in speech) the formation of speech sounds; the quality of clarity of speech sounds.

attention span: the length of time an individual can concentrate on something without being distracted or losing interest.

auditory discrimination: the ability to hear and perceive differences between sounds that are similar, but not the same, as *p* and *b*.

auditory perception: see auditory discrimination.

audiometer: an instrument used to test hearing.

basal readers: graded series of readers traditionally used in reading instruction; beginning readers use short words and simple sentence structure; vocabulary and sentence length and structure become more complex as the grade levels advance.

basic education: a course of study in which the basic tools of reading, arithmetic, and writing are acquired; frequently applied to adult education classes.

big books: books printed with large type, with the pages frequently as large as 18 by 24 inches; these are used when the teacher reads to the class or group, so that each child may see the page at a distance.

blend: the fusion of two sounds smoothly, so that each one is heard distinctly; the fusion of several sounds to form a word.

classics: literature that is widely appreciated, and that has, or is expected to, be appreciated for many years to come; for example, ALICE IN WONDERLAND, or THE SNOWY DAY.

compound word: a word that is made up of two or more words, such as baseball, firefly.

concept: an idea; the concept may explain how a specific thing is classified, as the concept of color relates to red, green and blue; it may deal with an abstract thought like honesty or loyalty.

configuration clue: a clue based on the general shape of the word; recognizing the shape, the reader may read the word.

consonant: a letter that represents a speech sound produced by the closing or narrowing of the mouth or throat, as *b, m, s.*

consonant equivalents: the two or three possible sounds for the same consonant, as in *s, c, g.*

consonant blend: two or three consonants sounded together, in which each of the sounds is still heard distinctly, as *str* in street.

consonant digraph: a combination of two consonants producing a single sound. In some cases, one consonant of the combination is heard, as in *ck, kn, wr, gh, gn, wh*; in others, an entirely new sound is produced, as with *ch, th, sh, ph.*

context clues: clues used to figure out the pronunciation and meaning of an unfamiliar word through the meaning of known words in the sentence or paragraph surrounding it.

cursive writing: writing in which the letters are connected; usually called handwriting.

decoding approach: an approach to beginning reading instruction which emphasizes sounding out the written message. Phonics and linguistic methods both use a decoding approach.

derivative: a word composed of a root word plus a prefix or suffix.

developmental reading: reading instruction designed to teach the reading skills systematically. The term is usually applied to reading instruction for the new learner, as opposed to remedial reading instruction, which is for students who have failed to acquire the necessary skills in a developmental reading program.

diagnosis, reading: an analysis of a student's reading competence and the exact nature of his reading skills and deficits. Reading diagnosis also attempts to determine the cause of the reading disability, and to suggest remedial treatment.

diagnostic check-list: a list of skills involved in the process of reading, in which the student's skills and weaknesses are recorded.

diagnostic test: a test designed for and evaluating individual strengths and weaknesses in reading.

dialect: a special variety of a language in which the words, usage, and pronunciation are characteristic of specific localities.

digraph, consonant: see consonant digraph.

digraph, vowel: see vowel digraph.

diphthong, or vowel blend: a combination of two vowel sounds that blend to become one. Both sounds are blended together. The common vowel diphthongs are *oi, oy, ou, ow, ew.*

directional confusion: inability of the reader to move the eye consistently from left to right; this results in reversals in reading, for example, reading *was* for *saw.*

discrimination, auditory: see auditory discrimination

discrimination, word: the ability to distinguish one word from another.

dominance, lateral: the preference for use of one side of the body over the other, as preferring the right hand, the right eye, the right foot.

dyslexia: medical term for reading disability, now widely used by educators as well.

emergent reader: a term used to describe the child as a "developing" reader at every age, beginning with infancy.

ESL: English as a Second Language.

experience chart: a printed or handwritten chart recounting an experience of the student in the words of the student. Although the term chart is used because this is a tool traditionally used in classroom instruction, it is equally useful with the individual learner in remedial instruction.

expected grade placement: the grade m which students of the same chronological age are usually found. For example, expected grade placement for a six-year-old is first grade; for a fourteen-year-old, it is the ninth grade.

eye-span: the amount of written material that can be perceived by the eye in one fixation.

families, word: groups of rhyming words containing identical word elements, as in *bat, hat, fat, cat, rat.*

figurative language: words and phrases that contain figures of speech, not to be interpreted literally, as for example, idioms and metaphors.

flash cards: cards on which letters, words, or phrases are written or printed; they are used for rapid drill, in arithmetic as well as in reading instruction.

frustration reading level: see Reading level, Frustration.

functional illiterate: the reader who reads below the fifth-grade level. In an industrial society, this reading level is inadequate for vocational competence in any occupations but those on the lowest economic level.

heteronym: words that have identical spelling, but different meanings and pronunciations.

holistic: emphasizing the importance of the whole and the interdependence of its parts; in education, the interdependence of the individual's interests, social, environmental and emotional status, and learning to learn.

homograph: a word that is spelled exactly the same as another, but is different in derivation and in meaning: as *sewer* (for waste disposal) and *sewer* (one who sews).

homonym: a word that sounds the same as another, but which differs in meaning and sometimes in spelling; *as to, too,* and *two*.

homophone: words that sound the same, but have different spellings and meanings.

idiom: an expression that cannot be understood literally.

Initial Teaching Alphabet (ITA): A 44-letter alphabet designed in England by Sir James Pitman to simplify the learning of reading. Each of the 44 letters in this alphabet stands for only one sound. Capital letters have the same shapes as small letters, instead of having different shapes, as do those in our alphabet.

independent reading level: see Reading Level, Independent.

instruction, individual: instruction given by a teacher to one person not in a group; one-to-one tutoring.

instruction, individualized: each student's instruction is based on a careful assessment of his needs; each student, individually or in a group, usually proceeds at his own pace.

instructional reading level: see Reading Level, Instructional.

invented spelling: spelling made up by the beginning reader, usually by sounding out the words.

kinesthetic instruction: instruction making use of the muscle sense and muscle movement. In reading, the kinesthetic sense is involved when the student traces the outlines of letters and words.

Linguistics: the science of language. A method of teaching reading that emphasizes a decoding, or sounding-out approach.

look-say method: the sight method; learning to recognize a word by its shape.

manuscript writing: writing by hand in a manner adapted from the printed letter; each letter is separately shaped, in contrast with cursive writing, in which the letters are connected.

metaphor: a figure of speech in which a term is transferred from the object it ordinarily designates to describe something else; for example, "she eats like a bird."

method, experience: see experience chart.

method, kinesthetic: see kinesthetic instruction.

method, mirror: a method that involves using a mirror in which the reader reads the printed matter; this method is sometimes used for readers who make an extraordinary number of reversals.

method, phonic: teaching reading by associating the letters with the sounds they represent.

method, sight: teaching reading by having the reader respond to whole words rather than having him depend on the sounds of the letters.

method, whole word: see method, sight.

multisensory approach: an approach to teaching reading that makes use of all of the senses: visual (eyes), sight words; auditory (ears), phonic analysis; kinesthetic (sense of movement), tracing letters and words; tactile (touch), raised letters, letters on sandpaper.

phoneme: a small unit of speech sound, as *m* in *mat*.

phonetics: the science of speech sounds; the system of sounds of a particular language.

phonics: the study of the sounds that letters make; a technique of reading instruction.

phonogram: a letter or group of letters representing a speech sound.

picture clue: a picture illustrating written matter that provides a clue to word recognition and meaning.

prefix: a syllable added to the beginning of a word to modify its meaning.

readability: a measure of the reading difficulty of a passage, based on the length of sentence and the length and type of vocabulary.

reader, disabled: a reader whose level of reading competence is significantly lower than is expected of him.

reader, emergent: see emergent reader.

reader, retarded: see reader, disabled.

reading level: the school grade is equivalent to the reading level for that grade.

reading readiness: the level of developmental maturity the child must reach before formal reading instruction is expected to be effective. At this level, s/he is able to perceive similarities and differences in shapes, knows some of the letters, and probably already recognizes several words at sight.

reading, developmental: see developmental reading.

reading, remedial: see developmental reading.

reading, word-by-word: halting reading m which every word presents to the reader an obstacle that must be mastered before the next word is attacked.

reading level, frustration: the level at which reading skills are inadequate: the reading loses its fluency, and errors become more frequent than 5 in 100 words. The reader becomes tense and uncomfortable.

reading level, independent: the highest reading level at which one can read fluently and with a minimum of error without assistance.

reading level, instructional: the highest reading level at which one can read fluently under teacher supervision.

root word: the base word, from which words are developed by the addition of prefixes and suffixes, such as *move* in *remove, removing..*

schwa: the soft sound for any vowel in an unstressed syllable, as *a bout, penc il, lem on.*

sight word: a word recognized automatically, usually by its shape.

spelling, invented: see invented spelling.

structural analysis: analyzing a word by breaking it down into its parts (root, suffix, prefix); if it is a compound word, breaking it down into its component words.

scanning, or skimming: rapid reading to gain an overall impression, or to find specific information, overlooking details.

suffix: a letter or syllable added at the end of a word to modify its meaning.

syllable: a letter or group of letters representing a vowel sound; it may or may not contain one or more consonants.

syllabication: the process of dividing a word into single syllables.

synonym: a word whose meaning is similar to that of another word which is spelled and pronounced differently, as *large* and *big*.

tachistoscope: a device that exposes material for a brief period of time so that it must be read at a glance.

test, diagnostic: see diagnostic test.

TESOL: T eaching (Teachers) of E nglish to S peakers of O ther L anguages.

tool subject: a subject involving the learning of a skill that is necessary for the learning of other subjects: reading, writing, arithmetic.

trade book: a book published for sale through bookstores and book sellers; not a textbook or a reference book.

visual discrimination: the ability to distinguish likenesses and differences between shapes, particularly letters and words.

visual perception: see visual discrimination.

vowel: a letter representing a sound made with the mouth open. The vowel letters are *a, e, i, o, u* . Sometimes *y* is used as a vowel.

vowel digraph (or teams): combinations of two vowels, or a vowel followed by w, which represents a single speech sound: *ai, ea, ie, oa, ay, ea, oo, au, ei, ow, aw.*

word: a symbol of an idea; the smallest unit representing an idea.

whole language: an approach to the teaching of reading that provides a climate in which the learner is encouraged to explore and learn; reading, writing, listening and speaking are integrated.

whole word approach: see sight word approach.

word families: see families, word.

word wheel: a device used to practice in word attack skills. It consists of two circular cards clipped together, each containing different word elements.

word attack skills: word analysis.

workbook: practice book, in which the student writes, that provides drill material in the reading skills. Workbooks sometimes accompany the textbook; at other times, they are prepared independently in order to provide practice in specific skill areas.